BORN AGAIN NOW WHAT

JESUS

IS THE

RESURRECTION

JOSEPH BRICE

Joseph Brice

CONTENTS

Contents

Credits

BCMG (Bridging the Conscience between Man and God), Inc.

Joseph Brice

© 2025 BCMG
Kingdom Rights

6

Dedication

This is dedicated to all who belong to the Kingdom of God — to those who love the Lord and believe in Jesus Christ.

You've been lied on, betrayed, misunderstood, criticized, mocked, and talked about in the worst ways. But through it all… **you are still standing.**

Take heart. Keep walking by faith. Keep doing the will of God. Your perseverance has not gone unnoticed, and your reward is waiting — a crown of glory that will never fade.

Blessings and peace to you, faithful one.

"For I consider that the sufferings of this present time are not worthy to be compared with the glory which shall be revealed in us." Romans 8: 18

To my Kingdom Rights Family, you are relentless and dedicated to the mission. Thank you for your loyalty and countless sacrifices. Great is your reward!

To my beautiful wife,

I honor you first as a woman — a secure, radiant soul who knows exactly who she is and whose she is. You are loving, kind, thoughtful, strong, and gracefully adaptable to God's purpose for your life. You embody what it means to be a true woman of God.

I'm especially moved by the way you quietly slip away to spend time in prayer. Those sacred moments between you and the Lord are a beautiful testimony of your devotion. Your love for Him shines, and it draws others closer to His heart.

You are such a powerful encourager, a steady supporter, and a constant source of strength. For all you do, may God overwhelm you with blessings that exceed anything you've dreamed of.

I love you — fiercely, endlessly, and relentlessly.

To all of my children,

My prayer is that each of you will walk boldly in your purpose. That you'll take your rightful place in this world and help make it better. Before you were ever formed in the womb, God knew you. He spoke destiny over your life — listen for His voice, remember His words, and obey the one that speaks truth.

Don't let anyone or anything pull you away from that truth. It's the one thing you'll always have — eternal, unshakable, and alive. You were born for greatness. Never forget who you are or the foundation you've been taught concerning your God.

You are wonderfully made, full of beauty and purpose. Love is your inheritance — receive it, give it, and watch it return to you in unexpected, miraculous ways.

And remember this: **God has not forgotten you.**
Two things make a diamond — **pressure and time.**
Some of what you've endured wasn't meant to break you
but to shape you. Greatness takes time — and that's exactly
why you're still here.

Time is not your enemy. **Time is your friend,** so use it
wisely and strategically.

**"His kingdom come, His will be done on earth as it is in
Heaven…"**

Acknowledgment

First and foremost, I extend my deepest gratitude to my Kingdom Family all over the world! A special thank you to Kingdom Builders Academy and The International School of Ministry for their profound, life-giving teachings and solid biblical foundations. Your faithfulness and guidance have been instrumental in this journey. Thank you!

To every family who has lost a loved one—whether unexpectantly, suddenly, through sickness, disease, the Pandemic tragedies, or war—our hearts and prayers are with you sincerely. We honor your pain and the weight of your loss. Know this: there is no sorrow too deep for God to feel and no wound He cannot heal.

Take comfort in this truth: Those who have gone home to be with the Lord Jesus are not longing to return. While their love for you remains, the joy and glory they now experience far surpass anything this world can offer. They are truly celebrating in His presence—what a reunion it must be!

It may be hard to grasp, but once you enter eternity, you will understand that *there truly is no place like Home.*

To all believers, be encouraged. This world is not our home —we are just passing through. Keep the faith. Keep God first. And remember, when this life ends, eternity begins. What unspeakable joy awaits us!

Live to live again...

Introduction

Before the cross, before the empty tomb, before the thunder rolled and the veil tore—there was a garden—a man made from dust and a choice that changed the world. Through Adam's disobedience, sin entered humanity. Death, once a stranger, became our inheritance. From that moment, the curse of sin ruled over every soul, generation after generation. The Apostle Paul wrote in Romans 5:12, "Therefore, just as sin came into the world through one man, and death through sin, and so death spread to all men because all sinned."

But God did not leave us without hope. "Therefore gird up your loins and your mind, be sober, and rest your hope fully upon the grace that is to be brought to you at the revelation of Jesus Christ; as obedient children, not conforming yourselves to the former lusts, as in your ignorance; but as He who called you is holy, you also be holy in all your conduct, because it is written, "Be holy, for I am holy.

And if you call on the Father, who without partiality judges according to each one's work, conduct yourselves throughout the time of your stay here in fear; knowing that you were not redeemed with corruptible things, like silver or gold, from your aimless conduct received by tradition from your fathers, but with the precious blood of Christ, as a lamb without blemish or spot. He indeed was foreordained before the foundation of the world but was manifest in the last times for you who through Him believe God, who raised Him from the dead and gave Him glory, so that your faith and hope are in God." *1 Peter 1:13-21*

From the moment of the fall, God set in motion His divine plan—one that would culminate in the life, death, and resurrection of Jesus Christ. Where Adam failed, Jesus would prevail. Through one Man's obedience, the curse would be broken.

Paul continues in Romans 5:19: "For as by the one man's disobedience the many were made sinners, so by the one man's obedience the many will be made righteous." Jesus is the Second Adam, the Redeemer, the spotless Lamb of God who took away the sin of the world.

His resurrection is not a side note to the gospel—it is the crown jewel. Without it, the cross would be a tragedy, and our faith would be in vain. "If Christ has not been raised, your faith is futile; you are still in your sins" (1 Corinthians 15:17). But Christ *has* been raised. He has conquered sin, death, and the grave.

When Jesus rose from the dead, He didn't just get up—He changed everything. The grave lost its claim. Death lost its sting. The curse lost its power.

The resurrection was foretold in prophecy: "For You will not abandon my soul to Sheol, nor will You allow Your Holy One to see decay" (Psalm 16:10). Jesus Himself declared in John 2:19, "Destroy this temple, and in three days I will raise it up." And He fulfilled every word.

The empty tomb is more than a symbol. It is a declaration of our justification (Romans 4:25), future resurrection (1 Corinthians 15:20–22), and eternal hope. Because He lives, we live also.

Before Jesus rose, those who died in faith rested in what Scripture calls Abraham's Bosom, or Paradise (Luke 16:22). It was a place of peace, but not yet Heaven. When Jesus died, He descended into the lower parts of the earth and proclaimed victory (1 Peter 3:19). He emptied that place and led the righteous into the presence of God (Ephesians 4:8–10).

Now, after the resurrection, there is no more waiting. Paul declares in 2 Corinthians 5:8, "To be absent from the body is to be present with the Lord." The veil is torn. Heaven is open. The blood has been applied.

One of the greatest previews of Jesus' resurrection power was found in the story of Lazarus. In John 11, Jesus arrives at the tomb of His friend, who had been dead for four days. But before He calls Lazarus forth, He makes a declaration that still echoes through time: "I am the resurrection and the life. He who believes in Me, though he may die, he shall live. And whoever lives and believes in Me shall never die."

Death was reversed with one command—"Lazarus, come forth!". But unlike Lazarus, who would one day die again, Jesus rose never to die. His resurrection is eternal, glorious, and victorious.

Through His resurrection, we have passed from death to life, from curse to blessing, bondage to freedom. This is not just history—it is your inheritance.

Jesus is the Resurrection and the Life. Believe in Him, live in Him, allow Him to live in you, and Rise with Him. The same resurrection power is in you if you have His Holy

Spirit!

Love Like Him!

Lead Like Him!

Live Like Him!

Reference

Dear Reader,

Thank you for joining me on this journey of truth, hope, and eternal life in *Born Again: Jesus Is the Resurrection*. I wrote this book with one burning message in my heart: **Jesus Christ has forever changed the destiny of humanity through His death and resurrection.** The Bible tells us that through one man's disobedience—Adam—sin entered the world, and with it came death, separation, and a curse that touched every soul born after him (Romans 5:12). That disobedience did not just affect Adam—it affected us all. Because of the fall, we were born into a world stained by sin, held captive by spiritual death, and under judgment.

But God, in His great mercy, sent Jesus—the Second Adam, the Lamb without blemish—to undo what the first man broke. Where Adam disobeyed, Jesus obeyed. Where Adam brought death, Jesus brought life. Through His sacrifice on the cross, Jesus took our place, bore our punishment, and made a way for us to be reconciled to God. Scripture says, *"For as by one man's disobedience many were made sinners, so by one man's obedience many will be made righteous"* (Romans 5:19). Because of Christ, we are no longer under the penalty or power of sin. We are no longer cursed. We are no longer separated. Through faith in Jesus, we are justified, made new, and brought into the presence of God.

Before the resurrection of Jesus, those who died in faith waited in Abraham's Bosom—Paradise—a place of rest, but not yet Heaven. But when Jesus died, He descended and declared His victory. He emptied that place and led the captives free (Ephesians 4:8–10). And now? There is no more waiting. The veil is torn. Heaven is open. To be absent from the body is to be present with the Lord (2 Corinthians 5:8).

This book is my humble offering to proclaim that truth. Jesus is not just a figure of history—He is the Resurrection and the Life. And because He lives, we live also.
I pray that as you turn the pages, you won't just read about theology—you'll encounter the living Christ, the One who paid it all so we could live again.

In Christ's love and truth,
Joseph Brice
Author, *Born Again: Jesus Is the Resurrection*

From The Author 2

I feel deeply compelled and inspired to write this book, intentionally grounding it in Scripture to support each message shared. If you're not a believer, I hope these words will help you see who Jesus truly is. And if you are a believer, I pray this strengthens and deepens your faith.

Jesus is the Resurrection — the heartbeat of our faith and the cornerstone of the Church.
Without His death on the cross and triumphant resurrection from the grave, humanity would be lost in sin, without hope and redemption. Every promise of salvation, every word of grace, and every breath of eternal life hinges upon this divine act of love.

In ***Born Again: Jesus Is The Resurrection,*** I explore the profound price Jesus paid to reconcile us to God. He took upon Himself the full weight of our sin and shame, willingly laying down His life so that we might live—not just in this life but forever in His presence. His blood became the atonement, His cross the altar, and His resurrection the doorway to eternal life.

For those who believe, who honor His death, burial, and resurrection, there is a gift beyond measure: forgiveness, freedom, and everlasting communion with the Father. But for those who reject His offering and turn away from the grace extended through Christ, there will come a day when they must stand before Him — not as Savior, but as Judge — and give an account for their denial of His sacrifice.

This message is not just theology. It's life. It's truth. It's the gospel. And it's the heart of everything I've written in this book.

Why We No Longer "Rest in Peace" After Jesus' Resurrection

Before Jesus' death and resurrection, the souls of the righteous—those who died in faith—went to a place the Bible refers to as *Abraham's Bosom* or *Paradise* (Luke 16:22). It was a place of comfort and peace, set apart from the torment of Hades, but still not Heaven. The full access to God's presence had not yet been made possible because the final atonement for sin had not been completed.

When Jesus died on the cross, He descended into Hades—not to suffer, but to proclaim victory (1 Peter 3:18–19). In that moment, He led the righteous souls out of Paradise and into the presence of God, fulfilling what had long been awaited (Ephesians 4:8–10). This act marked the end of the "waiting period" in the grave for the righteous. Now, because of Christ's finished work, believers who die do not go to a holding place. As the Apostle Paul declared, *"To be absent from the body is to be present with the Lord"* (2 Corinthians 5:8). Heaven is now open. There is no more need to "rest in peace" awaiting redemption—we enter immediately into the glory of God through Jesus Christ, the Resurrection, and the Life.

The Fall Through One Man — Adam's Disobedience

The statement originates from **Romans 5:12**:

"Therefore, just as sin came into the world through one man, and death through sin, and so death spread to all men because all sinned." (ESV)

This verse refers to **Adam**, the first man, whose disobedience in the Garden of Eden (Genesis 3) brought sin, spiritual separation, and death into the human experience. Theologically, this is known as the **Doctrine of Original Sin**—the idea that all humanity inherits the sinful nature through Adam. Because of Adam's fall, all were born into sin and subject to its curse, including physical death, spiritual death (separation from God), and the bondage of a fallen nature.

The Curse of Sin and Death

The curse affected all creation after Adam and Eve sinned (Genesis 3:17–19). Humanity was now subject to:

- **Physical death** (Genesis 3:19)

- **Spiritual separation** from God (Isaiah 59:2)

- **Moral weakness**, making us enslaved people to sin (Romans 7:14–24)

- **Condemnation under the Law**, which revealed sin but couldn't remove it (Romans 3:20; Galatians 3:10)

Paul puts it this way in **Romans 6:23**:

"For the wages of sin is death, but the gift of God is eternal

life in Christ Jesus our Lord."

The Second Adam — Christ's Obedience and Redemption

Paul continues the comparison in **Romans 5:18–19**:

"Therefore, as one trespass led to condemnation for all men, one act of righteousness leads to justification and life for all men. For as by the one man's disobedience the many were made sinners, so by the one man's obedience the many will be made righteous."

Jesus is often referred to as the **"Last Adam"** or **"Second Adam"** (see **1 Corinthians 15:45–49**). Where Adam failed, Christ succeeded. Through His perfect obedience—even to death on the cross—Jesus fulfilled the Law and satisfied God's righteous judgment (Philippians 2:8; Matthew 5:17).

His **death** paid the penalty for sin, and His **resurrection** broke the power of death. Through faith in Him, believers are no longer under condemnation (Romans 8:1), the curse (Galatians 3:13), or the dominion of sin (Romans 6:14).

Freedom from the Curse

Galatians 3:13–14 beautifully explains this:

"Christ redeemed us from the curse of the law by becoming a curse for us—for it is written, 'Cursed is everyone who is hanged on a tree'— so that in Christ Jesus the blessing of Abraham might come to the Gentiles so that we might receive the promised Spirit through faith."

This redemption is not just about escaping punishment—it's about **new life**, **justification**, and **reconciliation with God**. Through Jesus:

- We are **made righteous** (2 Corinthians 5:21)

- We are **born again** into a new nature (John 3:3–6; 2 Peter 1:4)

- We are **sealed with the Holy Spirit** and guaranteed eternal life (Ephesians 1:13–14)

- We are now **under grace**, not law (Romans 6:14)

Theological Summary

- **Original Sin**: Sin entered the world through Adam, and all humanity inherited a fallen nature.

- **Federal Headship**: Adam and Christ each represent humanity. In Adam, we die. In Christ, we live.

- **Substitutionary Atonement**: Jesus took our place on the cross, satisfying divine justice.

- **Justification by Faith**: We are declared righteous by trusting Jesus' finished work, not our own efforts.

- **Sanctification and Victory**: Through the Holy Spirit, we are being transformed and no longer bound by the power of sin.

We have been given *all power* over the enemy through the authority of Jesus Christ. Walk boldly, but walk wisely. Be

wise as a serpent—discerning, strategic—and never substitute productivity for prayer. Don't let busyness or entertainment distract you from the One who longs for intimacy with you. The Father desires your time. He desires **you**. Make space for Him—not out of obligation but out of love. Draw close to God, and He will draw close to you. Pray—not as a ritual but as a lifeline. Prayer is your portal to power, peace, and the presence of the Living God.

Know this: **the enemy may be permitted, but you've been empowered**.

Imagine, for a moment, what heaven is doing right now. Heaven is not just a concept—it's real. It has a location, an address, and a purpose beyond our comprehension. Now consider our tiny planet in the vast expanse of the universe. It's challenging to grasp. Yet everything we need to survive and thrive has been carefully crafted for beings of flesh—us —and every living creature that shares this world.

We live under the law of gravity, but the rest of the universe does not seem bound by it. Why is that? Does gravity apply to the soul, or is there another law tied to sin and death at work? All flesh is destined to die, but our souls—our spirit —live on for eternity. The question is: where?

Why do we assume the universe is just empty "space," devoid of life, except for distant theories of aliens or monstrous invaders? From a biblical perspective, I believe the invasion has already happened. Fallen angels and demons—under the control of Lucifer, also known as Satan or the Devil—have already infiltrated our world. While we look to the skies expecting danger to descend, the truth is, it's already here. And Jesus exposed it.

Somehow, we've drifted back to the same state we were in before Jesus walked among us—before He defeated Satan and placed him and his followers beneath His feet and under the authority of the Church. But we have not been left powerless. Heaven has given us authority—light, and righteousness—to rule in this world. The Kingdom of God is not distant. It is near, and it is within. And we are called to rise in that power.

"Behold, I give unto you the power to tread on serpents and scorpions, and over all the power of the enemy: and nothing shall by any means hurt you."
— *Luke 10:19 (KJV.*

We are a spirit, have a soul, and live in a body. This truth reveals the divine order of our being. The spirit is our eternal essence—breathed directly from God. Our soul— our mind, will, and emotions—processes the world around us, and our body is the temporary vessel that allows us to function in the natural realm. Though our outer man—this flesh—may wear down, the inner man is being renewed **day by day** (2 Corinthians 4:16). Life may leave us in broken places, but we do not remain there. *I will not die where you left me.* What tried to bury me didn't realize I was a seed.

See, a seed in isolation has potential, yes—but **potential alone doesn't produce a harvest**. The moment the seed is sown—buried in the earth, under pressure, in darkness—it begins to awaken. Purpose begins to push through the pain. The seed must die to itself to bring forth life. So, too, must we die to the flesh, to the limitations of our carnal thinking, in order to live in the fullness of God's resurrection power.

The flesh is flesh, but the spirit is spirit (John 3:6). While we are spirit beings—eternal, awakened, and reborn through Christ—we require a physical body to operate legally. That's divine protocol. Even Jesus, the Word made flesh, had to be born of a woman to fulfill His earthly mission. You are not just passing through this world—you've been sent here on assignment. Resurrection power isn't just about life after death—it's about life *right now*. You are coming out of this; whatever you may seem stuck in, keep the faith and never give up. What God planted in you will not stay buried. It will break through. It will rise. It will manifest.

If Jesus is not the Son of God, The Messiah, The Resurrection, then who was he? Why would the "powers that be" of the entire world agree to start time over? Why? What need was there to mess with time…to change time? People rarely can agree on anything without controversy because we are naturally opinionated. There's an innate nature of choice, so we exercise our rights to choose whenever and whenever it's allowed. So, we vote, or if we disagree, we protest.

Time for the entire world and civilization, as they would know it, was about to change forever, and no protest? I'm talking about every nation, every government, every race, every culture, around the entire world, was given notice about "TIME," and it is about to start over and…nothing? Jesus was tried, condemned, convicted, and executed as a criminal. Let's take away religion for a minute. He was executed by "Hanging Until Dead, Gas Chamber, Electric Chair, and Lethal Injection; these are just a few examples and methods of execution you may be familiar with: those convicted of a crime worthy of death and sentenced to die. Jesus was sentenced to die! Well, the Crucifixion was the

Roman Government's method of execution.

When he came to this world, he was on a schedule. He came to work, and when he was finished, he died. He came on purpose, to fulfill his purpose. "No man takes my life; I lay it down, and if I lay it down, then I will pick it back up again," Jesus said. John the Baptist called him " the Lamb of God, who comes to take away the sins of the world."

During the period that Jesus was crucified, it was Passover. According to the Law of Moses, they offered up blood sacrifices from sheep or lambs as the Atonement for their sins. Question: Why would the Israelites (Jews) stop offering a blood sacrifice for their sins, according to the Law of Moses? What offering can they give God? Who could they offer up to God in their place, according to their law, or anyone for that fact? Answer: Jesus is the Lamb of God who came to take away the sins of the World. He was and is the last and only sacrifice ever needed for the atonement of humanity's sins.

If Jesus is not the Messiah, Why would the entire World and the "Powers that be" agree to start time over to the whole World in honor of this man? Why wouldn't the Roman Empire (Government) or Caesar as an Emperor give themselves such a timeless and immortal honor, with time starting over?

Every time we schedule an appointment, go by calendar dates, celebrate holidays or birthdays, and just during day-to-day events, we acknowledge Jesus. Whether in knowledge or ignorance, believing or not, we recognize Jesus as Lord, even if we are not serving him. Time we started over in honor of this man, this God, who walked this earth. This is why I propose questions and answers in this book concerning B.C and A.D. and where they came from. We all know that the World is not 2000 plus years old. Every time we start a new calendar year, we are in celebration of his birthday date and his death date.

Jesus is presently sitting in Heavenly places, above all things which he created. God put it in the hearts of men to do his will. Why didn't the Devil stop time from starting over? The answer is that we cannot stop God. Blessed are all people who have accepted Jesus as Lord.

Kingdom is not a competition …it is supposed to be a completion. Yes, we strive for excellence and to be our best! But, at no time do we tear anyone down in the kingdom for us to come up. God will judge us. We are to love one another if nobody else ever gives us love. We are to be a people of love…not lust. When God sends people into your life, he does not send them to compete with you; he sends them to help you complete your purpose and fulfill your destiny. If they are competing with you, He did not send them, nor are they operating in the Spirit of God.

Unfortunately, some people are married to their competition! Sometimes, when people can't control you, they seek to sabotage or destroy you… that's OK as long as you recognize it. The Bible gives many examples, even what they did to our Lord Jesus. Judas was one of Jesus' disciples (in which the Lord had plans for him to sit on one of the 12 thrones in his kingdom), but Judas began competing with purpose. Both Judas and Jesus ended up hanging from a tree. Judas's hanging saved nobody, including himself, but on the other hand, Jesus's hanging saved the entire world of believers and Himself!

The enemy seduced Judas into believing he could use Jesus for a "come-up," but instead, he lost his place with God and his soul. If God called you, no one can take your place… even if they steal your position. Your place in God is secured! Some people have been sent as assassins for your purpose. Know this; you are well equipped for the fight; just put on your whole armor of God (Ephesians 6: 10-19). Be skillful with the WORD, your sword, and don't fight without your Shield (faith). Stand against that enemy and know who you are fighting! Recognize the Devil, even when he speaks through someone you may respect or even love.

This does not mean they are the Devil, but he can speak through others to reach us. When we shut him down through them, he attempts to speak directly to us in our minds. Remember, the Devil is a spirit and is desperate! Please don't play with him, directly or indirectly. He is venomous and lethal if not checked!

We have been given *all power* over the enemy through the authority of Jesus Christ. Walk boldly, but walk wisely. Be **wise as a serpent**—discerning, strategic—and never substitute productivity for prayer. Don't let busyness or entertainment distract you from the One who longs for intimacy with you. The Father desires your time. He desires **you**. Make space for Him—not out of obligation but out of love. Draw close to God, and He will draw close to you. Pray—not as a ritual but as a lifeline. Prayer is your portal to power, peace, and the presence of the Living God.

* * *

Know this: **the enemy may be permitted, but you've been empowered**.

You carry **authority** in Christ. Walk in it. Speak from it. Live through it.

You don't need anyone's approval or opinion to seek Jesus. Your relationship with Him is *personal*—built not on religion but love. So, know Him. Spend time with Him. Pour your affection on Him.

He is not only the Savior—**He is the Resurrection and the Life**.
And whatever has died in your life—hope, dreams, identity, purpose—He can resurrect it.

Your relationship with the Lord will be your greatest asset, unshakable foundation, and eternal security. Build it well and guard it dearly.

May the grace of our Lord Jesus Christ strengthen and sustain you. Be strong in Him. Keep the faith. And never let Him go. What a glorious inheritance we share—sons and daughters of the King, alive through the Spirit, sealed for the day of redemption.

To my fellow Kingdom citizens: peace and joy to you. I love you.
If not in this life… I'll see you when we get Home.

And if you're reading this and you've not yet surrendered your heart to Jesus, or you're unsure of your salvation—this moment is for you.

Jesus died for *you*.

Yes, *you*.

If you feel a tug in your heart or a stirring in your spirit, that's the Holy Spirit inviting you to eternal life. Jesus paid the price for your sins. He offers you freedom, forgiveness, and a future in His presence.

Don't wait. Don't wonder. Come home today.

Welcome to Born Again: Jesus Is the Resurrection.

With all love and faith,
Your eternal brother in Christ,
Joseph Brice

Something To Think About

Life is for the Living—so why wait to start?

What if the resurrection isn't a distant event but a living, present reality? In this thought-provoking journey, explore some of life's most profound questions: What happens when we die? Do we rest in peace, vanish, or is there more? Why does death exist, and what comes after? Perhaps most intriguing is what Jesus meant when he said, "I am the Resurrection and the Life"?

When Jesus arrives at Lazarus's tomb, Martha mourns her brother's death, saying he would have lived if Jesus had only been there sooner. But Jesus challenges her view of resurrection, proclaiming, "I am the Resurrection—not just an event but a person who brings life even beyond death. Through this powerful encounter, we discover that resurrection isn't merely an end-time event to anticipate but a living promise fulfilled in Jesus.

This book invites you to examine what it means to live with hope, to believe in God fully while you're still breathing, and to understand that life in Christ is both now and eternal. Why do we, as believers, mourn death as if we have no hope when we know that it's not the end for those who trust in Christ? Through faith, death becomes a doorway, not a dead end.

Journey through the truths of the resurrection with fresh eyes:

- **Is there really a Book of Life?** If so, whose names are written there?

- **Did Jesus truly defeat death?** What does it mean to have resurrection life within us today?

- **What awaits after death?** Are believers waiting in graves for a trumpet to sound, or is Jesus's promise immediate presence after death?

The resurrection of Jesus is the **cornerstone of the Christian faith**. It validates His divinity, fulfills prophecy, and secures eternal life for those who believe. Here are key passages and references:

◆ Foretold in Prophecy

- **Psalm 16:10** – *"For You will not abandon my soul to Sheol, nor will You allow Your Holy One to see decay."*
  ➤ This messianic psalm foretells Jesus' resurrection —quoted in Acts 2:27 by Peter.

- **Isaiah 53:10–11** – *"He shall see His seed, He shall prolong His days… He shall see the labor of His soul and be satisfied."*
  ➤ Even after being crushed, the Messiah would "prolong His days"—a sign of resurrection.

◆ Jesus Foretells His Own Resurrection

- **Matthew 16:21** – *"From that time Jesus began to show His disciples that He must… be killed, and be raised the third day."*

- **John 2:19–21** – *"Destroy this temple, and I will raise it up in three days."*
➤ He was speaking of His body—this was a direct prophecy of His resurrection.

◆ Eyewitness Accounts

- **Matthew 28:5–7** – The angel said, *"He is not here; for He is risen, as He said. Come, see the place where the Lord lay."*

- **John 20:19–29** – Jesus appears to His disciples and even invites Thomas to touch His wounds.

- **1 Corinthians 15:3–8** – Paul's summary of the resurrection appearances:
"He was seen by Cephas, then by the twelve… then He was seen by over five hundred brethren at once…"

◆ Theological Meaning of His Resurrection

- **Romans 4:25** – *"He was delivered over to death for our sins and was raised to life for our justification."*

- **Romans 6:9** – *"Christ, having been raised from the*

dead, dies no more. Death no longer has dominion over Him."

- **1 Corinthians 15:17–22** – *"If Christ has not been raised, your faith is futile… But Christ has indeed been raised from the dead, the first fruits of those who have fallen asleep."*

- **Philippians 3:10–11** – *"That I may know Him and the power of His resurrection…"*

🪦 Lazarus' Resurrection: A Sign and Foreshadowing

Lazarus' resurrection is recorded in **John 11**. This miracle is unique—not only in power but in timing and purpose.

◆ Key Scriptures

- **John 11:25–26** – *Jesus said to her (Martha), "I am the resurrection and the life. He who believes in Me, though he may die, he shall live. And whoever lives and believes in Me shall never die."*

- **John 11:43–44** – *"Lazarus, come forth!"*
  ➤ After four days in the tomb, Lazarus is raised by the direct command of Jesus.

◆ Symbolism & Significance

- **Foreshadowing:** Lazarus was resurrected *to die again*, but Jesus' resurrection was *to eternal life*. Lazarus' return from the grave points to the greater resurrection—Christ's victory over death itself.

- **Proof of Authority**: This miracle directly precedes the Passion Week and shows that Jesus has **power over death**, reinforcing His identity as the Messiah.

- **Glory to God**: Jesus intentionally delayed going to Lazarus to show God's glory through the resurrection (John 11:4).

◆ Connection Between the Two

🪦 Lazarus' Resurrection: A Sign and Foreshadowing

Lazarus' resurrection is recorded in **John 11**. This miracle is unique—not only in power but in timing and purpose.

◆ Key Scriptures

- **John 11:25–26** – *Jesus said to her (Martha), "I am the resurrection and the life. He who believes in Me, though he may die, he shall live. And whoever lives and believes in Me shall never die."*

- **John 11:43–44** – *"Lazarus, come forth!"*
  ➤ After four days in the tomb, Lazarus is raised by the direct command of Jesus.

◆ Symbolism & Significance

- **Foreshadowing**: Lazarus was resurrected *to die again*, but Jesus' resurrection was *to eternal life*.

Lazarus' return from the grave points forward to the greater resurrection—Christ's victory over death itself.

- **Proof of Authority**: This miracle directly precedes the Passion Week and shows that Jesus has **power over death**, reinforcing His identity as the Messiah.

- **Glory to God**: Jesus delays going to Lazarus intentionally to show the *glory of God* through resurrection (John 11:4).

◆ Connection Between the Two

Jesus' raising of Lazarus was a divine preview of what was to come. But unlike Lazarus, **Jesus' resurrection was eternal**. He did not come back to mortal life—He conquered death and was glorified.

Jesus' raising of Lazarus was a divine preview of what was to come. But unlike Lazarus, **Jesus' resurrection was eternal**. He did not come back to mortal life—He conquered death and was glorified.

This book also reveals a personal testimony from the author, Joseph Brice, of life beyond this life. In vivid detail, the author shares extraordinary encounters beyond the physical realm, experiencing a place prepared by God alone. Despite skepticism and lost relationships, this truth stands unshaken: life is beyond this life.

Through scriptural insights and personal revelation, this book will challenge you to rethink death, life, and the very nature of resurrection. Resurrection is not an event we wait for—it's a person we know, living within us, transforming every moment. Are you ready to live fully, with resurrection life as your reality?

Open this book and discover what it truly means to be alive in Christ—now and forever.

CHAPTER ONE
Born Again Now What?

The Power and Privilege of Being Born Again

To be *Born Again* is not just a spiritual concept—it is a divine transformation that brings us into God's Kingdom as cherished members of His family. As born-again believers, we are no longer outsiders but are adopted as God's children and granted the full rights of heavenly citizens. But do we truly grasp the depth of what it costs for us to be redeemed? Though salvation is a free gift, it came at the highest price —the life of Jesus Christ, who bore our sins so we could be restored to right standing with God.

All that's required of us is to *repent*—to turn away from our sins that separated us from God—and to *believe* and *receive* the gift of salvation through Jesus. This gift is not exclusive; it is available to *everyone* who believes, regardless of their past. Choosing Jesus means choosing life —*eternal life*, peace beyond understanding, and freedom from the burdens of this world. We can live with purpose, hope, and joy when we recognize that this world is not our true home and know we belong to a greater, everlasting Kingdom.

It is important to strengthen your relationship with your Heavenly Father. You can achieve this by praying, fasting, reading, and meditating on His word day and night, no matter what. When we are Born Again, we become children of God. He then spends time with us through His word and presence, seeking Him. He abides with us and prepares a place for us. As we grow, having Him with us should become our norm.

Communicating with God in the face of the many temptations surrounding us is essential. If you observe people passionate about their faith, you will notice that individuals often try to undermine that passion, even within the church. The church is not the kingdom itself but rather a community of people who belong to the kingdom. However, counterfeit versions and a black market will always exist, just like anything that holds value. The church is no exception."

It is important to take to heart the warnings that Jesus taught and gave to His disciples on many occasions. Failure to understand how much the devil wants to bring you back into his kingdom and work for him may lead him to use anyone or vessel to achieve your frustration with the church, people, and eventually God if you are not adequately equipped. Many people do not understand this and leave the church in significant percentages. While some make it back, others, like Judas, do not.

Listen to what Jesus tells His disciples and how this applies to us as His followers and in this generation, *"When an unclean spirit comes out of a person, it goes through arid places seeking rest and does not find it. Then it says, 'I will return to the house I left.' When it arrives, it finds the house unoccupied, swept clean, and put in order. Then it takes seven other spirits more wicked than itself, and they go in and live there. And the final condition of that person is worse than the first. That is how it will be with this wicked generation."* **Matthew 12:43-45 NIV**

There are people on earth who may hold beliefs contrary to God. However, it is important to remember that they were not always this way. Some may even say, "I used to go to church, but now I'm done with that. They made me believe everything was a sin. I want to do what I want to do." What happens is that when people stop praying and believing due to disappointments, their spiritual life becomes empty. God cleanses our hearts and souls, casting out unclean spirits when we get saved. Our hearts become a house filled with the things of God.

The unclean spirit that previously lived in you is now homeless and may have been with you since childhood; this spirit has occupied your soul. These are principalities…former princes from the kingdom of God who were cast down. *"Put on the whole armor of God, that ye may be able to stand against the wiles of the devil. For we wrestle not against flesh and blood, but against principalities, against powers, against the rulers of the darkness of this world, against spiritual wickedness in high places."* **Ephesians 6:11-12**

These spirits know the principles of the kingdom and how they work, whether good or evil if adequately utilized. Their job is to disqualify an individual, sowing seeds of doubt and ultimately turning to unbelief. Doubt is not a sin, but unbelief is; anyone can doubt, and that's a seed, but unbelief is the result of doubt, which is uninterrupted and becomes unified with evil and reckless thoughts turned into actions. The fruit of the seed of doubt has become the fruit of unbelief. Seed is sown into the mind, but unbelief comes from meditation on it until it matures and produces evil fruit, which can only happen if it is in the heart. You must believe the lie for the devil to work it and use you against the things of God and His will.

Now that God's belongings are no longer in your house, which He cleaned (the heart), the unclean spirit checks on you like an ex because he could not find anyone like you. You would listen to, entertain, and make him feel comfortable with his uncleanness; he misses home. He returns to check on his old address, which is your heart, and finds it available.

He is so excited at the thought of moving back in that before someone gets the individual to seek God again, he gets reinforcement, seven other spirits dirtier and more wicked than he is. He cannot afford to lose his house again; they have entered and taken over. This kind of person will find it hard to pray, read the Bible, go to church, and focus on the things of God that used to bring them joy that came so naturally. They will not only have no desire to pray and read God's word but will get irritated at the thought of seeking God all over again.

This is what makes it so very hard for the backslidden Christian. I used to be you, and I was sick and tired of that devil and those demons. I found myself doing things I would have never imagined. It took me years to figure this out, but I did it with God's grace, mercy, and help. One day, I cried out to the Lord for help because I knew this wasn't me; I wouldn't do these things. People mock people when they say, "The devil made me do it!" not all are lying.

When you struggle to find time to pray and read God's word, it could be a sign that you risk losing touch with your spiritual self. Prayer is a means of communicating with God, and the enemy seeks to sever this connection between you and your spiritual family. It's worth considering that things might have turned out differently if Judas had prayed instead of chasing after money. Instead, he led the enemy to Jesus while he was in the anointed place of prayer, the Garden of Gethsemane, where he earnestly sought God's guidance.

If Judas had not stopped praying, he would not have allowed doubt to turn into disbelief. Why? Judas wanted a king, prosperous, and notoriety, and Jesus was taking too long. Whatever your plight, the devil is constantly knocking at your door to see if your place is available again. Judas was saved (first stage) but didn't stay long enough to mature and be converted; there's a difference. Peter denied Jesus but remained for the next stage, which was being converted. Therefore, He became the apostle Peter rather than" the son of perdition." Don't allow the enemy to rob you of your next with God. Stay with God; in a thousand years from now, you'll be glad you did. Imagine where Peter is right now compared to Judas.

* * *

As Christians and believers, we have the Holy Spirit within us and, therefore, should not struggle with doubts about eternal life, the existence of angels or demons, or supernatural encounters with God. When we were born, we inherited a rebellious and contrary nature towards God due to Adam's sin of disobedience. This sin has separated us from God, our Father, and threatens our eternal life. It causes harm and robs us of peace, joy, and wholeness. Being Born Again gives us a new start and restoration of all things lost, especially our relationship with God.

The family of God and His kingdom is not something you can join; you have to be born into it. To understand the realm of royalty, you have to have royal blood. Kings are not elected; they are born. Born a king, raised as a prince with the understanding that the ultimate is becoming the king of rule. We are God's Royal Priesthood, kings and priests only ordained by God.

The power of being Born Again is that Jesus' blood becomes ours. When He died on the cross, our blood became His, and His blood dominated. By enslaving our place, He allowed us to take His place as a king. Jesus knew exactly what He was doing, and His resurrection made Him the first of His kind. When we see Him, we will become beings of light and perfection, just like Him. So, don't let anything discourage you from your belief in Christ. Whatever you may be going through, your best days are ahead. Being Born Again gives the believer the power to become children of God by blood. Let the redeemed of the Lord say, "So!"

When we are born again, it's a spiritual birth, and we inherit the spiritual nature of God. It is the primary reason for you not fitting in with others, especially those who have not encountered being born again. This is the clash of two different natures, characteristics, and kingdoms. As Being Born-Again, you have been snatched from the devil, his darkness and kingdom, because he no longer has a legal right to you. Sin gives the devil legal rights to your life. Operating in a sinful nature without resistance grants him the authority to be your god.

Receiving the Holy Spirit is our Comforter in our infancy stage and continues with us as we grow in grace. Still, as we mature in God, we should experience its power and ability to lead, guide, and connect us to God, angels, and eternity without restrictions marked by time. Christ should be at the helm of our existence. During his ministry, Jesus spoke about the availability of the kingdom to those who believe. He explained that there are three stages to gaining access to the kingdom. The first stage is that it is "at hand," which means it is available to you. The second stage is "upon you," meaning you have gained access and are experiencing the benefits of the kingdom, such as healings, deliverances, and miracles. The third stage is that the kingdom is "now within you," which means that you are a part of it and that the supernatural part of God is in you.

However, despite this, many Christians struggle to

believe other believers when they claim to have had visitations from angels or Jesus. This is perplexing because, as believers, we are part of the kingdom, and Christ and the angels are in it. Why wouldn't angels, or any other beings from the kingdom who serve God, be available to believers? Angels are appointed to us for protection and service, but it's important to remember not to worship them. We should honor and respect them as servants and messengers of God and recognize who they are in the kingdom, but our worship should be directed only to God.

Jesus said, You will see greater things than this, I assure you and most solemnly say to you, you will see heaven opened and the angels of God ascending and descending on the Son of Man [the bridge between heaven and earth]. **John 1: 50-51 AMP**

In the Bible, the first time Jesus spoke about being "Born Again" was to a Pharisee, a leader in Israel who was respected and known as a teacher in Jerusalem among the chief priests. His name was Nicodemus. It's interesting because this priest was considered a holy man who taught people about God. But Jesus told him that he needed to be born again. The priest didn't understand what Jesus meant and asked if he was supposed to go back into his mother's womb. Jesus explained that being born again meant being spiritually reborn, not physically. He was telling the priest that, even though he was a spiritual leader, he was too focused on physical things. Jesus reminded him that as a leader of Israel, he should know the importance of being spiritually minded and being born again.

* * *

Some bishops, pastors, and leaders have been saved for many years but have become infected with an arrogant spirit of religion. As a result, they do not feel the need to repent and be born again, even though it is precisely what they need to do. They may know how to do church and maintain religious practices, but they cannot see the kingdom of God, just as Nicodemus could not. Despite all the things Jesus did in his ministry, he never cast out a spirit of religion.

The religious person must denounce the spirit of judgment by humbling themselves to God and asking for forgiveness for attempting to usurp God's authority over His people. It requires surrendering oneself to God to invite Him into their hearts. God does not coexist with the devil. Many preachers operate from their anointing rather than God's glory. Satan deceives them into believing that God has not rejected them due to their anointing. However, this means that they will not enter heaven upon their death.

It is important to constantly examine our hearts for pride, regardless of how long we have been a part of a church community. We should repent and ask for God's transformation to make us new. We can pray and say, "Lord, please forgive me for my sins and allow me to be born again." This prayer can open our eyes to the truth and reveal God's true nature. Remember, the church is the people and not the building. We should focus on serving others to serve God rather than just attending services. The ultimate goal is to be a part of God's kingdom.

* * *

If you genuinely love God, humbling yourself before Him will be honorable. However, if you have the spirit of Lucifer inside you, it will enrage you. Have you ever wondered about the fate of the religious leaders who lied about Jesus and manipulated the law to have Him condemned and crucified? Are they at peace, sitting at the table with Jesus in heaven, or in a holding cell in Hell waiting for their court date to be taken before The White Throne Judgment? What do you think… I would like to know your opinion on this matter.

It's not on record that he openly told a thief, a murderer, a liar, a drunk, or any other sinner because they did not wrestle with theology and religious studies. These people were hungry and thirsty for God and needed his help; they were ready to receive God without contest. When sinners accept God and receive His Spirit, this is a spiritual new birth. They are born again, even if they don't understand what has happened to them or know what it's called.

What Jesus left on record for us is that the most complex people to humble themselves and receive God holistically are those who have studied God and hold high positions of spiritual authority in churches and other facilities where they can be used to teach people about a God they have not experienced or encountered. This kind of leader will teach that the Holy Spirit was a thing of the past and encounters we read about in the Bible happened back then, but God does not operate like this in the present day.

* * *

Like Nicodemous, they have not had a rebirth from God, and neither are they a part of God. These false teachers may as well teach God that He is dead if He cannot do in this generation what He did in past generations; know this about God: He is God of all generations, and "there is nothing too hard for God!" Why go to church in the first place if God has lost His power and is the God of the dead?

Many pastors and leaders have never been born again, although they teach and preach to congregations regularly; he said this to the so-called "holy man. This would be equivalent to Jesus talking to a Bishop, Pastor, or Pope in our day and time. In essence, Jesus was telling him he needed to start over. You have studied God, learned about God, and carried God's word, but you don't know God. Nicodemus was confused about who Jesus was, even though he saw manifestations of the Holy Spirit, which he studied in the Tora and Prophets, as signs of the coming of the Messiah.

Jesus also taught him the difference between the kingdom and religion, attending services versus being a servant of God, one who is willing to serve the people rather than esteeming himself above people looking to be served. Jesus lets him know why it was so hard for him to understand and see God when it is right there in his face. You can join a church, temple, or even a ministry, but you must be born again to be in the kingdom of God; the kingdom is not something or a place you can join or become a member of. Although Nicodemus saw scriptures being fulfilled that had been prophesied many years prior, such as where the Messiah would be born, a little town called Bethlehem, being a Nazarite to the Lord, being born of a virgin, the son of David, being rejected by his people, healing the sick, opening the eyes of the blind, being a shepherd of love and compassion to a loss and left people, one who would answer all their questions and solving eternal mysteries concerning God. He would bring God to the people without reservations. Jesus did all these things at this point, and the leaders continued not to believe.

The coming of the Messiah was the very foundation of this people, and the religious leaders heard about these things happening even if they did not witness it with their own eyes; they had enough witnesses to know whether Jesus was an impostor. These religious leaders are struggling with accepting Jesus as the Messiah because he's not what they imagine. Don't miss what God has for you because it does not appear or look like you imagined your answer.

Could this be the answer to our prayers? Jesus was their answer, but they were looking for something else. They waited on another Messiah, another fulfillment that fit the narrative and their imagination of what God should look like, what the Son of God should look like, what the Messiah should look like, or what about the coming of the Son of Man or the Son of God would have we imagined?

Jesus did not come into this world to save the devil and his followers. He came to expose the devil's works so he couldn't hide anymore. He gave his life and died to save humanity, to save us who all believe in him and put our trust in him, and then he will take us home to his kingdom, which is our kingdom. You may wonder how people can lie, know the truth, and even go to court, put their hand on the Bible, and swear in the name of God that they are telling the truth, the whole truth. Nothing but the truth and then lie; what makes a good liar?

It is said that a great liar knows the truth, the whole truth, and uses it to their advantage. However, we must understand that the devil also uses people to spread lies. In such situations, Jesus advises us not to be anxious about what we say, for our Heavenly Father will guide us. We should not be surprised when we encounter people who lie effortlessly, especially in court or when it concerns money or other worldly things. Those who do the devil's work are his children and speak his language. Jesus wants us to understand this and not be shocked by the works of the devil, but instead, we should strive to destroy his works and be separated from him. When you become a born-again Christian, you may experience people turning against you and hating you. This is because you now belong to a different kingdom, the kingdom of God. You have a spiritual birthmark given to you by God, and the devil knows this mark.

Whether you are a child, an adolescent, a young adult, an adult, or a senior, your age doesn't matter. You may go to work the next day after encountering God on Sunday and giving your life to Christ, and people will start treating you differently without even mentioning that you gave your life to Christ. They may start withdrawing themselves from you because you are now a different creature spiritually. A different creation is almost like being an alien; others may look at you, but they don't understand you. They may feel uncomfortable around you, and you may be left out of groups you used to be a part of. You may wonder why you're not invited to lunch or shopping with them anymore, even though you haven't done anything wrong.

This is why the people of God need to embrace one another. Your true family consists of those who have been born again, not those who are merely faking it or attending church out of habit. This is why the movement in the Book of Acts was so remarkable. Despite being persecuted and hated, the believers loved one another. They understood that the world hated them because it first hated the true prophets and Jesus. This world is our proving ground, where we determine what kingdom we belong to and who will be our God and Father.

Jesus was sent to expose the devil who has been hiding on this earth and committing all kinds of corruptible deeds. We were unaware of his actions for a long time. However, now that he can no longer hide, he is angry. If you are Born Again, you must stop trying to fit in with the world because you will never belong there. Instead, as a born-again Christian, you belong to God and his kingdom. It's important to understand that the devil has his kingdom and followers who will spend eternity with him. These individuals engage in evil deeds, and they destroy communities, people, families, and even churches. As a result, they are different from us, and we must not entangle ourselves with them, trying to be accepted.

They are of another creation. They are the children of darkness and will never do what's right, no matter the consequences. They are obsessed with buying good things, although they are evil. They don't have a good heart or good intentions; they are selfish and wicked, and they are doing the will of their father, which is the devil.

No matter what you do, they will never love or accept you. If they do not accept Jesus as they have, the fight is on; their assignment given to them by Satan is to get them to denounce God as Judas did. You will have to denounce God, divorce him to get things from the devil on a whole other level, and get on his payroll; he wants to be your source, and this is why weak people sell their souls.

If we're not careful, we might worship a dressed-up and made-up lost soul hiding behind material things purchased with money. Some people are dying while they are living and selling their souls for a compliment. This is all they live for: to be praised and worshipped. Wanting too many people to like them that's too much power to give to any potential enemy. This is the Devil's greatest weakness. He desires your praise and worship; he desperately wants to be God. Being born again and taught God's word without false doctrine will open your eyes to the kingdom's truth. Don't be afraid of what you see. It's not the devil, and you are not crazy.

We think we know people, maybe not as well as we believe; *Jesus said, "Do not think that I have come to bring peace to the earth. I have not come to bring peace but a sword, for I have come to set a man against his father, and a daughter against her mother, and a daughter-in-law against her mother-in-law. And a person's enemies will be those of his own household. Whoever loves father or mother more than me is not worthy of me, and whoever loves son or daughter more than me is not worthy of me. And whoever does not take his cross and follow me is not worthy of me. Whoever finds his life will lose it, and whoever loses his life for my sake will find it."* **Mathew 10: 34-39**

This applies to every one of us: If you have not been born again, then according to Jesus, you are considered an enemy of God. On the day of judgment, Satan will present evidence against you, and you will be judged accordingly. Therefore, it is essential to understand the significance of being born again and its importance.

When you are born again, and others are not, loved ones who belong to the other kingdom can hate you without understanding. It does not matter whether they attend church; to be considered true family, they must belong to the same kingdom as you. I am a living testimony to this truth; those who do not belong to God's kingdom can turn on you. Human effort cannot fix this situation; it is beyond our control. Only God has the power to remedy it.

Jesus is the truth himself; that's why he always spoke truthfully. It's unsurprising if people you thought loved you hate you. They might have been pretending, and their father could be the devil if they hadn't accepted God in their lives. This is not just a ceremony; it's about loving each other and being a part of God's eternal family. Love never fails, so try to see things through the eyes of the Holy Spirit and use discernment to understand what's happening. You'll notice that God is absent in the eyes of those against you. This doesn't mean that we should become judgmental, but we should be aware of what's happening around us so that we don't give in to the pressures they put on us. Jesus has exposed the enemy so the devil cannot hide from the Holy Spirit. There are two kingdoms; if you look carefully, you'll see who belongs to which.

I witnessed people who used to preach, pray, fast, and lay their hands on people turned away from God because He took too long to bless them the way they wanted to be blessed. They became offended and disappointed because God did not show up for them in a materialistic way. He did not give them the pleasures of the flesh like they imagined the blessings should have brought them.

They wanted to use God rather than allowing God to use them, and for this reason, they turn on God and His people; they will hate you for loving the Lord and preaching the gospel; they will hate you for choosing God over them, they are deceived into thinking this is a competition as if they can compete with God. They will hate you for even talking about God or mentioning His name, and that's why we must be careful that we do not allow the world to turn our relationship with our Heavenly Father into a religion. Where you can't talk about religion, you can talk about your Father. If you're Born Again, Now What? Where do I go from here? What do I do with my days as a new Born-Again Believer? What do I do with my time because everything is different?

Being Born Again is powerful because while we cannot choose our natural parents, we get to choose our Heavenly Father and accept Christ as our Savior. Looking around humanity, we see every human being was born through a woman. It is a universal truth that every human, regardless of race, creed, religion, politics, education, or occupation, entered this world through a woman. However, when we go to heaven, we will all have one thing in common - we came through God through His spirit. This is what unites us in the Kingdom of God. If you're not, you are an alien and don't belong there.

Everybody is not going to heaven because they do not belong there. Evil does not belong in heaven, nor can sin exist there. This is why Lucifer and the other angels were kicked out; they were kicked out before their sins had a chance to manifest; the evil hidden in them is being exposed every day in this world by way of every race and generation. Some are worse than others, but manifestations for sure. It would be in comparison to trying to live in a place where there is no air. If you carry or supply your air, eventually, the air will run out. Evil cannot survive in heaven because it has nothing to feed it, nothing to nurture it. There was nothing in heaven to promote evil, darkness, sins, or transgressions.

Now that you're born again, pray consistently, read God's word, study God's word, meditate on His word both day and night, gain strength, and grow in grace. Mature in God to the point that the devil knows he will get hell messing with you, as he did with Jesus, He shouted at the top of his voice, "What do you want with me, Jesus, Son of the Most High God? In God's name, don't torture me!" For Jesus had said to him, "Come out of this man, you impure spirit!" Then Jesus asked him, "What is your name?" "My name is Legion," he replied, "for we are many." And he begged Jesus again and again not to send them out of the area. **Mark 5:7-10 NIV**

Your Holy Ghost is like a fiery furnace, a fury not to be played with.

Read God's word until you see yourself in the word, be confident, be stable, and unmovable in God's love no matter what the enemy tries to do to you. His works against you are temporary; you will have the victory and the last word. Your enemies will be cut down like grass, so pray for them and leave it in God's hands. Love God with all of your heart; let no one or anything change that, and those who hate you hate the God that's in you; there's nothing you can do about that. Don't hate them back. You may have to keep your distance. People will leave you because you will not leave God, and that's how powerful being born again is.

People will leave you; spouses may divorce you or cheat on you with someone less than you or maybe someone who used to be close to you because the devil is working through them, trying to get a carnal, worldly, and ungodly reaction from you. In hopes of you going back to your old life, which is the Old Serpent called the Devil and Hell. Do not react but pro-act. Don't be predictable.

It would be best if you weren't shocked at their behavior because you said I did a good thing. Yes, you did. I gave my life to Christ. Yes, you did, and welcome to the family of God; being Born Again is the greatest thing you can do in your life because you establish who your Father is, where your home is, and who your family is. When you're Born Again, you belong to the family of God, and I would like to say welcome to the family of God. You are Born Again; Now What?

"Put on the whole armor of God so that you can stand against the devil's schemes. Our struggle is not against flesh and blood but against the rulers, against the authorities, against the powers of this dark world, and against the spiritual forces of evil in the heavenly realms.

Therefore, put on the whole armor of God so that when the day of evil comes, you may be able to stand your ground and, after you have done everything, stand. Stand firm then, with the belt of truth buckled around your waist, the breastplate of righteousness in place, and your feet fitted with the readiness that comes from the gospel of peace. In addition to all this, take up the shield of faith, with which you can extinguish all the flaming arrows of the evil one.

Take the helmet of salvation and the sword of the Spirit, which is the word of God. And pray in the Spirit on all occasions with all kinds of prayers and requests. With this in mind, be alert and always pray for all the saints. **" Ephesians 6:11-18**

Live for God, be like God, love like God, be excited, and look forward to loving people while spreading the good news of the kingdom until it's your time to leave this world. When you leave this world, you will be reunited and united with your actual family, the family of God, those who have been praying for you and cheering you on because they preceded you in this world and fought so they understand how challenging it can be. To the Born Again Believer, remember this: death is not your enemy or punishment; death is your servant, your transportation, your Uber to heaven, rejoice you are going home.

In all fairness, we cannot expect people, on average, to understand us when we become born again when we see on record how a priest didn't. We have much more information and testimonials on the subject, but most importantly, we must understand it's spiritual. Being misunderstood is common, but it doesn't become evil until people attempt to destroy you or your faith in

God. People becoming aggressive and destructive is a sign of negative influence. Seek support from like-minded individuals. Surround yourself with other Born Again Believers.

This is vitally important for the new believer. Two kingdoms are at work here, and the true kingdom of light is already victorious over the want-to-be kingdom of darkness. The enemy lives a fantasy of being god and a king having his kingdom. He desperately desires to be God; therefore, he will practice on the weak, wicked, insecure, and those who are thirsty for prestige and power. They have no love for you! Everything he blesses you with is linked to destruction.

Do you understand that Lucifer never wanted to be a father? He's too selfish. He destroys children; he's the devil, the adversary, the destroyer of relationships, families, and children. He wanted to be God, not a Father! When Lucifer was in heaven, he saw God as king, Rich, and glorious beyond measure, The God of everything; he did not see God as a Father. God had everything but a son; children from his own body understand that everything God created came into existence by his spoken word, but when he looked around, He had no Son!

One of God's names in the Bible was "Ancient of Days." Abraham is considered a type and shadow of God. As an older man, Abraham was blessed with wealth, servants, land, possessions, and all the luxuries money could buy. However, he didn't have a child, a son of his flesh and blood from his own body. He was raising his nephew, his brother's son, who had passed away, as his son, but he knew that Lot was not his biological son. Abram longed for a son that he could call his own, one that came from his own body.

Abram had everything a man could ever want except for a son. After his brother's death, he became a father figure to his nephew Lot, but he still longed for his child. God appeared to Abram in a dream and told him to leave his father's house, promised him a son of his own body, and led him to a new land that He would give to him and his seed; he was seventy-five. Abram and his family were idolaters at the time when God appeared to him; they were worshipers of idol gods, gods they could see, touch, and handle. But somehow, Abram believed this new and invisible God's promise to him, even though he didn't know him then. God promised Abram a son, which Abram wanted above all the things that he had.

Abram shared with his father and family the encounter with God and decided to obey this God and go to an unknown land that He would lead him to. He left everything behind, including his family, friends, and home. However, some people, including his nephew, Lot, were willing to accompany him. Can you imagine the feelings and emotions they must have experienced knowing Abram was convinced he had heard from a God? Considering his age, they must think Abram is losing his mind. The fact that he and his wife have never been pregnant. Abram leaves his security and experiences numerous hardships and significant losses, including famine. Abram continued to follow the new God he was becoming familiar with; this was the beginning of a man who would be famously known for having faith in God and become biblically known as the Father of Faith.

It's certainly possible that Lot may have suggested that his uncle should let the dream go and be satisfied with him as a son. Abram must have appeared foolish to Lot and his followers, who were so old. When you are waiting on the promises of God, and it may seem impossible, this is the making of a miracle if you have faith in God. Don't let the chatter of unbelievers discourage you; stand on what God has promised you even if you have to let those you love go. Your life and purpose is hinged on your faith. If you surround yourself with those who are against what God has promised you, they are against God; just let them go!

Years later into this journey, after many trials and tests, Abram and Lot had disputes due to issues involving followers, possessions, prosperity, and company. There was great tension between Abrams's herders and Lot's herdsmen, even though Abram said to his nephew he didn't want bad blood between them so that he would separate himself from Lot for peace's sake. Abram said to Lot choose which way you will go, and I will go opposite you. Lot saw the beauty and watered land in the direction of Sodom and how it was well watered, "like the garden of the Lord, like the land of Egypt." Lot took his wife, children, herders, and followers to journey towards Sodom and Gomorrah. Later, Lot gets into trouble in Sodom and Gomorrah and loses all his possessions.

* * *

The LORD said to Abram after Lot had parted from him, "Look around from where you are, to the north and south, to the east and west—all the land that you see I will give to you and your offspring forever. I will make your offspring like the dust of the earth so that if anyone could count the dust, then your offspring could be counted. Go, walk through the length and breadth of the land, for I am giving it to you." **Genesis 13:14-17 NIV**

The four kings seized Sodom and Gomorrah's goods and all their food; then they went away. They also carried off Abram's nephew Lot and his possessions since he lived in Sodom. A man who had escaped came and reported this to Abram the Hebrew. **Genesis 14:11-13 NIV**

Abram saved Lot from losing his wife, family, and possessions to the kings who fought against Sodom and Gomorrah. Abram went to war to save his nephew. After parting ways with his nephew Lot, Abram headed in one direction while Lot returned to Sodom and Gomorrah. They never saw each other again. Later, God would judge Sodom and Gomorrah, but Abram could not save Lot from the impending disaster. At one of the lowest points of his life, God visited Abram, who was grieving the separation of his nephew, whom he loved like a son.

After Lot and his followers left Abram, God

appeared to him in a life-changing way. God reinforced his covenant with Abram and told him he would become the father of many nations. God also promised that Abram's seed would be blessed and he would receive the land where he lived. At that time, Abram lived in Canaan, while Lot lived in Sodom and Gomorrah. Sometimes, we may have people we fight for in our lives, but they secretly fight against us. It's possible to love people who don't reciprocate the same love.

Abram's wife, Sarai, thought she was too old to have children. She suggested to Abram give her a son through her slave, Hagar. Maybe it's me who's hindering the covenant from coming to pass. So Hagar bore Abram a son, and Abram gave him the name Ishmael; he was eighty-six years old.

When Abram was ninety-nine years old, the LORD appeared to him and said, "I am God Almighty; walk before me faithfully and be blameless. Then I will make my covenant with you and greatly increase your numbers." **Genesis 17:1-2 NIV**

God appeared to him and instructed him on the practice of circumcision. God told him that His covenant would be marked in the flesh of males' private parts. This mark was a sign of God's covenant with Abram to separate him and his descendants from other people and nations. Abram was to teach his sons about God and the covenant they carry in their flesh, making it known to them that they were a chosen people. During this period in Abraham's life, God changed his name from Abram to Abraham and his wife's name from Sarai to Sarah. God commanded Abraham to be circumcised before he could conceive Isaac, signifying that they were his seed and had a covenant with God.

As God had promised, Abraham and Sarah gave birth to their son Isaac the following year. However, before they could have the child of the promise, they had to be tested and tried by God, proving that they were not the same people as they were twenty-four years before God first called Abraham. It took years of preparation for them to be ready and qualified by God to bring forth His promise. Abraham had to let go of trying to be a father to someone who didn't respect him as a father, and instead, he had to learn how to be a good and obedient son to God himself, setting an example for his son.

Meanwhile, God was planning to visit the city Lot was living in for judgment. God sent angels who appeared as ordinary men. They were sent to Lot's house; they represented God undercover. This was probably because Abraham interceded for Lot, although he was selfish and not pleasing to his elderly uncle. Certain people of the city came to Lot's house asking to see his guests, and Lot refused them; he offered two of his daughters instead to the men who wanted to have sex with his guests. Lot had four daughters in all. Understanding what God is about to do, Abraham asked, "Will you destroy the righteous with the wicked?" God eventually interceded for Lot and his family on Abraham's behalf, saying," I will spare the city if I can find ten righteous people there."

The angels tell Lot to run to the hills, save his family, and not look back at this city. Lot flees the town with his wife and two of his daughters. Eventually, the judgment of God falls on the city, and it goes up in flames. Lot's wife could not help herself and looked back and turned into a pillar of salt. She disobeys God, not knowing the consequences; I believe she looked back because of her two daughters who were left behind. This would probably be the reaction of any excellent mother, but the harsh reality is they were grown and decided to stay behind.

They may have felt ill toward their father Lot for giving them up so quickly and protecting guests over his daughters. They imagined what they saw and heard their father do against his uncle Abram. Lot's wife, family, and friends knew Abram was a good man and father to Lot in his absence. Abram was good to Lot and his family. Some men become fathers by mistake or sometimes entrapment, but Abraham wanted to be a father purposefully. He wanted to be a father more than anything and was willing to pay the price for it. This is why he was such an excellent father to his brother's son, as if he was his own. Competing with his uncle would ultimately cost Lot everything, including his family. Eventually, Lot would have children by his own two youngest daughters, and they would be sons. Lot was not a good person, husband, or father.

He probably made children because he thought his uncle Abram could not. He wanted to be more successful than his uncle. If not, he should have supported and protected his uncle, giving him added strength to wait on the promises of God, but instead, he caused Abraham grief and pain. Lot would never see his Uncle Abraham with his new name, life with his sons, or the promised land God gave him. Lot's pride kept him in that cave, living a life of incest and shame. He could have returned to his uncle and repented to start the relationship over. But because of his unrepented heart, he could not be trusted; God kept Lot away from Abraham.

However, Lot should have acted humbly and submitted to his uncle and God. He failed to see that Abram was more than just a man of greatness, but rather Abraham, the father of many nations. Who could see this in the natural? It takes faith to believe the impossible. God has bigger plans that extend beyond our lifetime, and we should trust Him rather than ordinary things. Although history proves it, Lot was a wicked man, and his uncle Araham's intercession is no doubt what saved him from being destroyed in the city.

Sometimes, we may be hurt by people that God takes out of our lives and have no clue they will never submit to God and change their wicked ways. Abraham did not want to believe this of his nephew, but he loved him so much. Being born again will open your eyes to the truth that although you love people, it doesn't guarantee they love you the same. Through Abraham's example in the Old Testament, love them anyway, but when they show you they cannot love you back, let them go, or they may destroy your faith in God.

Abraham is a type and shadow of God. Out of Abraham would come Isaac, and out of Isaac would come Jacob. The God of Abraham, Isaac, and Jacob. Out of the Father came Jesus; out of Jesus came the Holy Spirit. The Father, The Son, and The Holy Spirit.

Remember when Jesus answered the Pharisees and said, "Before Abraham was, I AM!" Before Jesus came, the covenant was in the private part of the flesh, but after Jesus Christ's Resurrection, the new covenant was in the private part of the heart. "No one can know the heart but God." Why? It is not meant for everyone to see because it is the private part of our soul and spirit. This is one of the main reasons that Salvation is the work of the heart, not the flesh. It is the place for God to dwell.

This is why Jesus said, "Behold, I stand at the door (heart), and knock: if anyone hears my voice and opens the door, I will come into him, and eat with that person, and they with me" (Revelation 3:20).

This is about a relationship, a consensual spiritual relationship. God will not force Himself on any of us, no matter how much He loves us; we must accept His love and reciprocate it. We are to grow in our relationship with God; this is the reason for a consistent prayer life, reading God's word, and assembling with other believers for encouragement and strength to know you are not in this fight alone.

Being Born Again gives your soul and spirit a new start; your flesh is the house they dwell in; your flesh is not born again; your spirit is. You are putting your flesh under subjection and authority to your new spirit and

Holy Spirit. You are one with God and value your relationship like a marriage. You are betrothed or engaged now; carry yourself in such a manner that you are spoken for. Do not allow the enemy to violate you and your covenant with God. The Holy Spirit is like your engagement ring; stay pure and faithful until your wedding day. The wedding happens when you leave this world and go to the world prepared for you from the foundations of the world.

Nothing in the past matters; you cannot change the past. Start your new life in Christ knowing you are married to Christ and your soul belongs to him; you are spoken for. You must remain loyal, dedicated, and faithful to God through Jesus Christ. To those who may not understand your new walk with God, the devil will continue on your trail because he wants you back. You were his slave and property by thief; he stole you from God in the garden, thief by deception. God cursed the ground for our sake, meaning the stuff our bodies are made of, not our soul and spirit.

Believers have so much to look forward to; you are the bride of Christ, not a harlot for the devil. DO NOT let the devil violate you! Stay with God!

Some people have played both sides and strayed from God. You cannot serve two masters; the devil understands this, even when we don't. They may have had a dedicated life to God, praying, reading the word, and being faithful to a church or ministry. Then you look at them, and they are doing things they have never done before. Some of the things are shocking to them as they are doing them. Some things are so terrible they will never disclose them to anyone; there are no secrets between them and the devil. We know God knows everything; this is why repentance is necessary; you can return to God no matter what you have done.

Again, you must be Born Again; don't play with the devil this time! God knows and sees you if you are reading this and know this is you and feel convicted. Just humble yourself to God and repent. There is no shame in what you've done. "We all have sinned and come short of God's glory." The shame is not telling it, repenting, and starting over with a clean slate. This is the power of being Born Again.

God may require you to expose that devil who had you in bondage as a declaration of your alliance with Christ and the kingdom of God. When you are born again, knowing who feeds you and what you eat is essential. This is spiritual, not natural. You have to eat right and grow in the truth of God's word to mature to the place where you become converted. Just because you are saved doesn't mean you are converted. Judas was saved being with Jesus but did not finish the course to be converted.

When you are converted, the devil has no authority over you; you are mature enough to exercise power and authority over him. You become like Christ; leaving God is the last thing the enemy or anybody can cause you to do, and you are sold out to Jesus. Judas cut a deal with Satan for thirty pieces of silver. If we do not overcome the lust of the eye, the lust of the flesh, and the pride of life, the devil knows he has a chance to turn us against God. Peter denied Jesus because he was not yet converted. Nothing surprises God; He knows what we are going through, but we are not alone. Look at what Jesus told Simon Peter before it happened,

And the Lord said, Simon, Simon, behold, Satan hath desired to have you, that he may sift you as wheat: But I have prayed for thee, that thy faith fail not: and when thou art converted, strengthen thy brethren. And he said unto him, Lord, I am ready to go with thee, both into prison and to death. And he said, I tell thee, Peter, the cock shall not crow this day; before that, thou shalt three times deny that thou knowest me. __ Luke__ **22:31-34**

Every human being in this world, regardless of race, creed, religion, sex, belief, or occupation, has come into existence from a man's seed and through a woman. It is undeniable that every person born in this world owes their existence in the flesh to a man and woman. Becoming a citizen of a new country involves complying with its laws, rules, and regulations. As an American citizen, you cannot dictate your country's laws to another country to gain citizenship. If you desire to become a citizen of the Kingdom of God, it would be wise to comply with the King's laws and be thankful for the privilege of being granted citizenship.

Now, there was a man of the Pharisees named Nicodemus, a member of the Jewish ruling council. He came to Jesus at night and said, "Rabbi, we know you are a teacher who has come from God. No one could

perform the miraculous signs you are doing if God were not with him." In reply, Jesus declared, "I tell you the truth, no one can see the kingdom of God unless he is born again. "

"How can a man be born when he is old?" Nicodemus asked. "Surely he cannot enter a second time into his mother's womb to be born!" Jesus answered, "I tell you the truth, no one can enter the kingdom of God unless he is born of water and the Spirit. Flesh gives birth to flesh, but the Spirit gives birth to spirit. You should not be surprised at my saying, 'You must be born again.' The wind blows wherever it pleases. You hear its sound, but you cannot tell where it comes from or where it is going. So it is with everyone born of the Spirit. "

*"How can this be?" Nicodemus asked. "You are Israel's teacher," said Jesus, "Do you not understand these things? I tell you the truth; we speak of what we know and testify to what we have seen, but still, you people do not accept our testimony. I have spoken to you of earthly things, and you do not believe; how will you believe if I speak of heavenly things? No one has ever entered heaven except the one who came from heaven–the Son of Man. **John 3:1-13***

Have you ever considered the power of being born again? Amazingly, we get to choose who our father will be. *"But as many as received him, to them gave he the power to become the sons of God, even to them that believe on his name: Which were born, not of blood, nor of the will of the flesh, nor the will of*

man, but of God." John 1:12-13

After Simon, now known as Peter, went to the upper room on the day of Pentecost and received the Holy Ghost with power, he was converted. Before this experience, Simon knew the Holy Ghost only as a comforter, not power. This experience taught him that we need both aspects of the Holy Spirit. He was never the same after receiving the Holy Ghost with power and boldness. He was addressed as Apostle Peter from then on. Many Christians get saved but do not complete the process of being converted and end up leaving, thinking it's too hard or not working. Many compromises, so they have one foot in and the other foot out, and for this reason, they do not have the power and authority over the enemy that Jesus gave us to have.

"But ye shall receive power, after that the Holy Ghost has come upon you: and ye shall be witnesses unto me both in Jerusalem, and in all Judaea, and Samaria, and unto the uttermost part of the earth." **Acts 1:8**

The Holy Ghost or Holy Spirit is meant to give us power, but unfortunately, many preachers and pastors have studied about it without ever experiencing it themselves. This is a problem for the parishioners because these pastors may discourage them from seeking this experience with God. Remember, Jesus died so that we could have His Spirit on earth. However, some pastors and teachers have been influenced by a deceptive spirit and try to convince people that having the Holy Ghost is no longer relevant.

Do not be misled by them!

Please note the following truth: The Holy Ghost and power are available to every believer until Jesus returns and takes all of his people out of this earth, leaving it to Satan for a thousand years. Do not allow anyone to reduce the power of God to speak in tongues, as this is a trick. Speaking in tongues is only one manifestation of the Holy Ghost, and exercising your power and authority over the enemy is what Jesus ordained you to do.

The enemy will use any method to deter as many people as possible from believing they can have authority over evil. False doctrines are preached and taught to weaken the Christian's faith in the supernatural power of God's spirit. Distractions and deception enable the devil to reign free. He has taken over our families, communities, and churches - because we are not operating in power and authority. We have become great worship producers, but not the power of worship. Therefore, if you are going to be a believer or Christian, you owe it to God and yourself to go all the way and do what Jesus commands, having His Holy Spirit. After all, He died for us to have these privileges.

Why is it difficult to understand when Jesus says we must be born again of the water (symbolic of the woman) and Spirit (God's seed)? In the Kingdom of God, every person who reaches there will only do so because they were "Born Again." This is the prerequisite to living in God's world, Heaven, which is eternal. For those who reject this, Heaven is not their home; in other words, they do not belong there—those who embrace God's word and are born again become part of the family of God.

Setting aside quality time to allow God to nurture and guide you is essential for strengthening your relationship with Him. You can grow in your faith by reading God's word, fasting, and praying constantly. As you consistently engage in these spiritual practices, you'll begin to mature in your faith and ultimately become a warrior for Christ. You will not be easily persuaded to indulge in immoral and ungodly things. If you love like Jesus, Live like Jesus, and Lead like Jesus. This will enable you to help save others and guide them towards becoming more like Christ...to change the world.

We were created initially to worship God; the enemy desires more than anything to pervert our worship by us worshiping him and material things; he's hiding behind many things we pursue in life to throw us off track. Being born again gives us a new slate; we are newborns who worship God as our Father. Anyone born of the Spirit will owe their life and existence to Jesus. Jesus said, ***"You cannot see the kingdom unless you are born again; you cannot enter the kingdom unless you are born again." I AM the Way, the Truth, and the Life; no one will come to the Father unless they come through me."***

Just as every human being who has ever come to this earth has come through a woman, so will everyone from this earth who will make it to heaven

come through Jesus! Who will you believe, the One who loved us so much that He came down from heaven to redeem us by unselfishly laying down His life for us, or the rebellious One who was eternally kicked out of heaven because of his selfishness, jealousy, hatred, and pride?

Jesus, the only One who came down from heaven to save us, says, "You must be Born Again."…Now What? Will you do it? Will you be born again? It's every person's choice as to who their eternal Father will be.

If you accept Jesus, You are Born Again into a new life, and that life is eternal…

CHAPTER TWO
B.C. - A.D.

What does BC and AD mean?

BC and AD are the terms used to describe the years "Before Christ" (BC means before Christ) and "AD" (In the Year of Our Lord).

AD stands for the years after Jesus Christ's birth, while BC stands for the years before. There is no year zero; only the year 1 BC, followed by AD 1. BC always comes after the year, and AD comes before the year.

What Year is BC and AD?

When we talk about the years BC, they go backward from year 0. So, the BC years get bigger as you go to the left on a timeline.

The AD years go forward to the right. Of course, our system of using BC notation didn't come about until centuries after the fact. There's no way folks in those days could have known they were living in the days of having the years go backward!

In most everyday communication, we don't even use AD. When we record the day/month/year, we list the year as part of the date. We use BC if we are talking about something that happened long ago. In everyday conversation, it doesn't come up too much. But you can't ignore the fact that the AD years started sometime. And there had to be a reason for it!

What does the Latin Phrase Anno Domini Mean?

Anno is similar to our English word Annual, which denotes a year. Domini means Lord (who dwells in dominion over all creation). But AD is an abbreviation of the original term, which was quite a bit longer. The original Latin phrase is **"Anno Domini nostri Jesus,"** meaning "In the year of our Lord Jesus Christ."This explains why AD is regarded as meaning "In the year of our Lord."Some folks guess AD stands for "After Death."

But this meaning is impossible for AD. If it were true, there would be an approximate 33-year gap between BC and AD, which would be unworkable. Another consideration is the abundant and dramatic historical and literary evidence of Jesus' resurrection. Jesus' death is a significant historical fact. But the many overwhelming historical facts surrounding **his resurrection** make Jesus' factual return to life after a horrible death very compelling. It's interesting to note the Gregorian calendar and the AD notation are not essential to the Christian faith and are not part of Biblical teachings.BC and AD do not appear in the Bible. They do make it much easier to understand history, though!

So, how did BC and AD happen?

The calendar we use today is solar. It's called the Gregorian calendar. It begins at the same place yearly in the Earth's orbit around the sun. It has become the world's standard calendar. However, the calendar of the ancients was a lunar calendar based on the moon's orbit around the Earth.

The Jewish calendar, still in use today, is an excellent example of a lunar calendar. So is the Chinese lunar calendar. This lunar system was exemplary in the early years of human history when everyone was looking forward. But in later years, it made the historian's job difficult. There was no direct record of the years, so it was tough if a historian needed to calculate the date of some important event. And as Western culture advanced, it became more important for commercial reasons to schedule events for future dates.

A change was in order, so a dynamic Roman monk of Scythian origin named Dionysius Exiguus devised this new system in 525 AD. Dionysius had an excellent reputation for scholarship. He was known for translating many critical Greek works into Latin for the Pope. The then-current calendar system used data from the era of Diocletian. Dionysius didn't want to give glory to Diocletian, a bloodthirsty Roman Emperor who had brutally persecuted and murdered Christians. Dionysius did his work over 500 years after the birth of Christ and left no record of how he made the calculations. Later, scholars found he was off by a few years, so the birth of Christ is currently listed as ~4-6 BC. Dionysius' small error is not a theological issue.

When Was AD First Used?
The birth of Christ remains the dividing line of world history, just as he intended. Dionysius' work took several hundred years to catch on one nation at a time until the entire world accepted his calendar system. The first written

records using this notation were by the English Priest Bede (Saint Venerable), who made numerous notations in 679, 692, 697, etc.

Why Do We Use BCE and CE?
[People Also Ask: "What are BC and AD now called?]
BCE stands for "Before the Common Era" (Before the Current Era), and CE stands for "Common Era" (Current Era), and both are substitutes for BC and AD. These terms date back to as early as the 18th Century.BCE and CE were popularized by people who were not Christians. They noted the very Christian nature of the BC and AD and that saying AD acknowledged the Lordship of Jesus Christ. Not everybody is willing to do that, so the alternates allow them to use more religiously neutral terms.

It's apparent to all that there must be a reason for the divide between BC and AD. Christians can accept the usage of BCE and CE by unbelievers without taking offense. However, this dividing line is the birth of Jesus Christ. There's just no avoiding it. We could easily say BCE and CE refer to "Before the Christian Era" and "Christian Era" since this dating system corresponds directly to the birth of Christ.

Birth Date of Jesus
In ancient times, the calendar began at the Regnal year one (the first year of their reign) at the coronation (crowning) of every new monarch. For example, we read about the history of the kings of Israel in the Old Testament, and there are references like this: "In the eighteenth year of King Jeroboam, Abijah began to reign over Judah." 2 Chronicles 13:1 The New Testament reads the same way

"In the fifteenth year of the reign of Tiberius Caesar..." (Luke 3:1a, ESV)

So, history began anew with the coronation of a new king. This is why we can pinpoint the birth of Christ down to a year. The Bible tells us the year in terms of those days. The equivalent Hebrew year of Jesus' birth (~4 BC) would have been ~3756-3757.

When **Jesus Christ was born, the Magi immediately recognized him as King**. Now, after Jesus was born in Bethlehem of Judea in the days of Herod, the king, behold, wise men from the East came to Jerusalem, saying, "Where is he who has been born **king of the Jews?** We saw his star when it rose and have come to worship him." Matthew 2:1-2, ESV

Now, we hear of the Magi and see the three men on camels in the nativity scenes and think it looks cute under the Christmas tree. But the Magi were powerful and influential men from a priestly caste of Persia who were not to be trifled with. Jesus' genealogy would have been on scrolls in the temple, so it was verifiable. And when the temple was destroyed in 70 AD, so were the genealogical records. So, any later claim by another cannot be proven.

Jesus Christ remains King of the Jews (Matthew 27:37), and when he returns, he will assert his kingship over the whole world. How appropriate, then, that we mark the years since his birth as the years of his reign, just as was done during ancient times for the earthly kings. Jesus' birth lies at the horizontal intersection of world history, and his death and resurrection lie at the vertical intersection of world history. This intersection of the horizontal and vertical is emblematic of his bridging the gap between man to man (Jesus is 100% man) and God to man (Jesus is 100% God).

If Jesus is not the Messiah, the Christ, why would the world who hated him agree to start time over in his honor? Especially those who do not believe. Where is Satan's power to stop this? Now you have those pushing the agenda to move related materials pointing to Jesus as the point of time and the Calder. How long did it take? Who was this person to cause such an upset in the world using love, peace, forgiveness, caring for the vulnerable and weak? He is the gift of God from Heaven—Emanuel, "God with us."

What will anyone say when they take their last breath and face this God? We do everything by the calendar and time. What will be your defense in the King's Court Room? Can your defense be that you have never heard of Jesus or that you have never used time and a calendar? This man came as a modest working-class carpenter or builder. He could have come as anything he chose to, but he came humble. He was rejected and despised.

Why would the Romans or any other being in power give this man such honor who was accused, convicted, and condemned to death by execution (crucifixion)? There is so much evidence of Jesus being the manifested presence of God right here on earth among his people. God loves his people, but the problem is that we need to love him back. Some people wish they could return and do it again, but they blew it. Don't take the chance by not accepting the offering Jesus has afforded us. If you don't know him, start today. Repent, confess to him, and take the rights that come with you as sons and daughters of the Most High God. One day, we will all give an account of our life on this earth.

Good or evil, we will be rewarded. We can submit and bow now or later. In his presence, you will find how powerless you are. People talk badly, but we will all witness how fear will grip those who are enemies of God like no other experience before. Nothing can compare to the reality of facing your creator and having charges against you because you believed a Devil over God.

For it is written, As I live, saith the Lord, every knee shall bow to me, and every tongue shall confess to God. (Romans 14:11) Wherefore God also hath highly exalted him, and given him a name which is above every name: that at the name of Jesus, every knee should bow, of things in heaven, and things in earth, and things under the world; and every tongue should confess that Jesus Christ is Lord, to the glory of God the Father. (Philippians 2: 99-11)

When you think about world history and timelines, God has always been in the picture. He is all-knowing. The prophets and prophecies all line up; some took generations to pass. When we think of a God who resides in eternity while we are here in time, hundreds, thousands, or even millions of years don't matter. He will eventually get to what his plans are. Even when people of power think they are fulfilling their vision, someone places it in that person's heart.

For God has put in their hearts to fulfill his will, and to agree, and give their kingdom unto the beast, until the words of God shall be fulfilled. (Revelation 17: 17)

* * *

God put His imprint on this earth, primarily through TIME! Second, minutes, hours, days, weeks, months and years...B.C.("Before Christ)" A.D. (Anno Domini, a Latin phrase which means " in the year of our Lord.")

No matter how Satan tries to change it in these last days, it's TOO LATE; the world has already been saying and living "in the year of our Lord," like it or not...

CHAPTER THREE
Follow Me

"Follow Me"

Where did we first hear this? Is this new, or is it a reoccurrence? We live in a world where it is trendy and a new normal through" Social Media" to follow someone. This generation is the most advanced in technologies and access to what used to be impossible. To this generation, God is granting access. Access to what—Secrets of His Kingdom? No other generation has seen more than this one. But, "To whom much is given, much is expected" (Luke 12:48). All of this knowledge-seeking will have rewards or consequences.

Follow me, the informal invitation. Jesus starts his ministry and goes to the Jordan River, where John the Baptist is baptizing and preaching one message, " Repent for the kingdom of God is at hand." He is not biased or prejudiced with his message... it's literally to everyone until he encounters The One! Jesus leaves his job as a builder and is compelled to get baptized. It is his submission to his called and ultimate purpose. Jesus was working and holding down a job just like us today. But, something is calling him to his destiny...to his purpose for being in this world. He leaves his family and job and heads down to the Jordan River to be baptist of John.

* * *

*Now John is at the Jordan preaching repentance and preparing for the coming of the One mightier than him. John is called the forerunner of Christ. Now, who is John? John is the son of Zacharias and Elisabeth, both of the Tribe of Levi. Zacharias was a temple priest, and Elisabeth was Aaron's daughter. Aaron, of course, was Moses's brother and the first established and ordained by God to be a Priest of Israel... a Levitical Priest. John was conceived in his parents' old age. Elisabeth was past the age of childbearing; John was their miracle baby. " For this is he that was spoken of by the prophet Isaiah, saying, "The voice of one crying in the wilderness, Prepare ye the way of the Lord, Make his paths straight" (**Mathew 3:3**) . "Behold, I will send you Elijah the prophet before the coming of the great and dreadful day of the LORD." (**Malachi 4:5**)*

*John was sent for one purpose: to prepare the people for the Lord. How is the preparation done? By way of repentance (to turn away from evil and return to God). The Bible in the Book of Genesis notes the first acknowledgment of sin or the separation from God. When Adam and Eve ate from the forbidden tree and its fruit, this caused their separation from God. Disobedience to God is the formula for separation. "For by one man's disobedience, many were made sinners, so by the obedience of one shall many be made righteous" (Romans 5:19). All disobedience to God is sin. "Where in time past ye walked according to the course of this world, according to the prince of the power of the air, the spirit that now worth in the children of disobedience" (**Ephesians 2:2**).*

John is gone! He is preaching a method unheard of,

especially by his peers. He walked away from church, leaving behind all natural riches and resources. Most people don't realize how rich the Levitical Priests were. John came from a well-to-do family. No one could make heads or tails about why John would go into the wilderness with nothing and live off the land as a vagabond. *"And the same John had his clothing of camel's hair and a leather belt about his waist, and his food was locusts and wild honey. (John 3:4)*

Although the priest preached for 400 years since the prophet Malachi's prophecy of one crying in the wilderness, when they see it, it's nothing as we imagined, though right there in our faces. It goes for truth even today. When someone comes along doing what preachers preach and teach about every day, he somehow shuns the poor and seeks the rich to hear.

John was sent to make the crooked way straight. John is considered to be the forerunner to Jesus Christ. Both of Jon's parents were very old when he was born, so I believe the loss of his parents was his sign to leave home because nothing was holding him there. He was the only child. John, by revelation, started preaching repentance and baptism. Many came to John and believed his message, but the Pharisees questioned him. They watched as the people followed John. They were wondering if he could be the Messiah, or could he be the one? Because John was one of them, a Levite, a Priest, and a descendant of Moses and Aaron, they were considering how to deal with John. John's stage was the wilderness, totally exposed to the elements, with no comfort or shelter. His message was without prejudice and bias across the board. *"Repent, for the kingdom of heaven is at hand (near)." This is he who was spoken of through the prophet Isaiah. "A voice of one crying in the wilderness, prepare the way for the Lord, make straight the pathway for him.*

John's clothes were made of camel's hair, and he had a leather belt around his waist. His food was locusts and wild honey. People went out to him from Jerusalem and all Judea and the whole region of the Jordan. Confessing their sins, they were baptized by him in the Jordan River. But when he saw many Pharisees and Sadducees coming to where he was baptizing, he said to them: "You brood vipers! Who warned you to flee from the coming wrath? Produce fruit in keeping with repentance. And do not think you can say to yourselves, 'We have Abraham as our father.' I tell you that out of these stones, God can raise children for Abraham.

The ax is already at the root of the trees, and every tree that does not produce good fruit will be cut down and thrown into the fire. "I baptize you with water for repentance. But after me will come one who is more powerful than I, whose sandals I am not fit to carry. He will baptize you with the Holy Spirit and with fire. His winnowing fork is in his hand, and he will clear his threshing floor, gathering his wheat into the barn and burning up the chaff with unquenchable fire."

Then came Jesus from Galilee to Jordan unto John, to be baptized by him. But John forbade him, saying, I have a need to be baptized by you and come you to me? And Jesus answered and said unto him, Let it be so now: for it is proper for us to fulfill all righteousness."Then John consented. And as soon as Jesus was baptized, he went up immediately out of the water: and, that moment the heavens were opened unto him, and he saw the Spirit of God descending like a dove, and lighting upon him: And lo a voice from heaven, saying, This is my beloved Son, in whom I am well pleased. **(Mathew 3:4-17)**

"Then Jesus was led by the Spirit into the wilderness to be tempted by the devil. The tempter came to him and said, "If you are the Son of God, tell these stones to become bread." Jesus answered, "It is written: 'Man shall not live on bread alone, but on every word that comes from the mouth of God.'" Then, the devil took him to the holy city and had him stand on the highest point of the temple. "If you are the Son of God," he said, "throw yourself down.

For it is written: " 'He will command his angels concerning you, and they will lift you up in their hands, so that you will not strike your foot against a stone.'" Jesus answered him, "It is also written: 'Do not put the Lord your God to the test.'" Again, the devil took him to a very high mountain and showed him all the kingdoms of the world and their splendor. "All this I will give you," he said, "if you will bow down and worship me." Jesus said to him, "Away from me, Satan! For it is written: 'Worship the Lord, your God, and serve him only.'"Then the devil left him, and angels came and attended him." **(Matthew 4:1, 3-11)**

Jesus sets an example for us on how to deal with the devil when you are called to a purpose. Instead of waiting for the devil to show up and tempt him throughout his ministry, Jesus went looking for him. That's pretty "gangster"! Jesus knew that Satan was the leader of his gang and was well aware of their capabilities, given that they received their training and gifts from him in heaven. Jesus, being the Word made flesh, had the power to resist the devil's temptations.

Note to the Five Fold ministers: If Jesus went to be tempted by the devil before he started his ministry, should we do so as well? Everything the enemy would bring to him in his ministry, he exposed him to the wilderness in private before he did ministry in public. In other words, if you don't get the victory in private, the devil will not respect you in public.

This is the reason so many are afraid of the devil. They know that they took the offer from the devil in private, so how can they **rebuke** the devil in public? So they say things like this, "I don't even want to mention his name," or let's not talk about the devil (most of the time…it's the enemy), but Jesus called this devil out. Jesus took no bribes or prisoners.

Jesus turned down every offer the devil made. Remember when the devil showed him the kingdoms of the earth and their glory? This means kingdoms of religion, government, and the world. The Pharisees were on the devil's payroll, but Jesus saw them along with the world kingdoms. Be sure, Pastors and church leaders, that you didn't get your stuff you're calling blessings from the wrong source. Fact Check: Are you allowed to rebuke Satan? Do you have the authority to cast out devils? Can you say "JESUS" without getting into trouble?

Jesus set people free, who wanted to be free everywhere he went, cast out devils, and embarrassed Satan and his demons. He showed his authority and power over all the enemy.

"Jesus returned to Galilee in the power of the Spirit, and news about him spread throughout the countryside. He was teaching in their synagogues, and everyone praised him. He went to Nazareth, where he had been brought up, and on the Sabbath day, he went into the synagogue, as was his custom. He stood up to read, and the scroll of the prophet Isaiah was handed to him. Unrolling it, he found where it is written: "The Spirit of the Lord is on me because he has anointed me to proclaim good news to the poor. He has sent me to proclaim freedom for the prisoners and recovery of sight for the blind, to set the oppressed free, to proclaim the year of the Lord's favor." Then he rolled up the scroll, gave it back to the attendant, and sat down. The eyes of everyone in the synagogue were fastened on him.

He began by saying to them, "Today, this scripture is fulfilled in your hearing." All spoke well of him and were amazed at the gracious words that came from his lips. "Isn't this Joseph's son?" they asked. Jesus said to them, "Surely you will quote this proverb to me: 'Physician, heal yourself!' And you will tell me, 'Do here in your hometown what we have heard that you did in Capernaum.' "

"Truly I tell you," he continued, "no prophet is accepted in his hometown. I assure you that there were many widows in Israel in Elijah's time when the sky was shut for three and a half years, and there was a severe famine throughout the land. Yet Elijah was not sent to any of them but to a widow in Zarephath in the region of Sidon. All the people in the synagogue were furious when they

heard this. They got up, drove him out of the town, and took him to the brow of the hill on which the town was built in order to throw him off the cliff. But he walked right through the crowd and went on his way." **(Luke 4:14-26, 28-30)**

Even Jesus couldn't do many mighty works there because of their **unbelief!** Sometimes, people are stuck with where and who they were before answering the calling. You will find that your most valuable time will be wasted on people who are stuck in your past. Satan will use them to hold you hostage to the old you. It doesn't necessarily mean bad; it's just not converted for the calling and purposes of God. We go through processing before placement.

Although Jesus may have been an excellent builder, it was part of his process, not his destiny. So don't allow anyone to bind you to your process; go out and evaluate your progress. So you don't need more **ANOINTING; you need a different crowd. Don't change your message; change your audience!** Jesus preached the same message but got unprecedented results because he was willing to leave his comfort zone—even his family. Don't be afraid to change locations and people if necessary. If you do what God has called you to, you may win your family later…but go! *"From that time on, Jesus began to preach, "Repent, for the kingdom of heaven has come near." As Jesus was walking beside the Sea of Galilee, he saw two brothers, Simon called Peter and his brother Andrew. They were casting a net into the lake, for they were fishermen.* **"Come, follow me,"** *Jesus said, "and I will send you out to fish for people." At once, they left their nets and followed him.*

Going on from there, he saw two other brothers, James,

*son of Zebedee, and his brother John. They were in a boat with their father, Zebedee, preparing their nets. Jesus called them, and immediately, they left the boat and their father and followed him. Jesus went throughout Galilee, teaching in their synagogues, proclaiming the good news of the kingdom, and healing every disease and sickness among the people. News about him spread all over Syria, and people brought to him all who were ill with various diseases, those suffering severe pain, the demon-possessed, those having seizures, and the paralyzed, and he healed them. Large crowds from Galilee, the Decapolis, Jerusalem, Judea, and the region across the Jordan followed him." **(Matthew 4:17-25)**

After this, Jesus and his disciples went out into the Judean countryside, where he spent time with them and was baptized. John was also baptizing at Aenon near Salim because there was plenty of water, and people were coming and being baptized. (This was before John was put in prison.)

Some of John's disciples and a certain Jew argued over ceremonial washing. They came to John and said to him, "Rabbi, that man who was with you on the other side of the Jordan—the one you testified about—look, he is baptizing, and everyone is going to him."

John replied, "A person can receive only what is given to them from heaven. You yourselves can testify that I said, 'I am not the Messiah but am sent ahead of him.' The bride belongs to the bridegroom. The friend who attends the bridegroom waits and listens for him and is full of joy when he hears the bridegroom's voice. That joy is mine, and it is* *now complete.*

He must become greater; I must become less." The one who comes from above is above all; the one who is from the earth belongs to the earth and speaks as one from the earth. The one who comes from heaven is above all. He testifies to what he has seen and heard, but no one accepts his testimony. Whoever has accepted it has certified that God is truthful. For the one whom God has sent speaks the words of God, for God gives the Spirit without limit.

The Father loves the Son and has placed everything in his hands. Whoever believes in the Son has eternal life, but whoever rejects the Son will not see life, for God's wrath remains on them." (John 3:22-36 NIV)

Look at how sly and messy the devil is; he had disciples thinking it was their idea to bring up the fact that the one John was on the other side baptizing. John spoke of Jesus the entire time he was baptizing. He even called Jesus *"The Lamb of God, who comes to take away the sins of the world."*

The devil tried to start a competition between the two and create strife. But see how John handled this situation. Unfortunately, many of our leaders have not taken the precious jewels from these two leaders. This was the beginning of where we get the denominational divide. The devil would use this throughout the growth of the church.

The mission was to save, and the purpose was to give birth to the church. Constantly, you will see followers go back and forth between followers of John and followers of Jesus. John was baptized with water, and Jesus later with fire. So, as you read the Book of Acts, you will hear the effects of the followers representing their denomination.

The very beginning of the Baptist church versus the Pentecostal Church. They both preached repentance and the kingdom and knew their purpose for being in this world. But, the devil continued to use weak people with hidden agendas to bring division in the church, and it took a toll on the early church and church to this day.

Some of John's followers remained faithful, even after his death. They would proclaim themselves proudly as John's followers, while others broadly declared Jesus as Lord and asked if they had received the Holy Spirit. The church continued to grow tremendously, even while being persecuted! Jesus said, ***"The gates of Hell will not prevail."***

These two leaders were of God, pure at heart, and sent by God, but only one will prevail. Only Jesus is the Resurrection and the Life. The same devil who came after Jesus in the spirit used people to continue to persecute the church but could not stop her.

We need to understand that there is no competition in the kingdom. We unite to complete the vision, not to cause division.

*"At daybreak, Jesus went out to a solitary place. The people were looking for him, and when they came to where he was, they tried to keep him from leaving them. But he said, "I must proclaim the good news of the kingdom of God to the other towns also because that is why I was sent." And he kept on preaching in the synagogues of Judea." **(Luke***

4:42-44)

The Cost of Discipleship

Jesus called his twelve disciples to him and gave them authority to drive out impure spirits and to heal every disease and sickness. These are the names of the twelve apostles: first, Simon (who is called Peter) and his brother Andrew; James, son of Zebedee, and his brother John; Philip and Bartholomew; Thomas and Matthew, the tax collector; James, son of Alphaeus, and Thaddaeus; Simon the Zealot and Judas Iscariot, who betrayed him.

These twelve Jesus sent out with the following instructions: "Do not go among the Gentiles or enter any town of the Samaritans. Go rather to the lost sheep of Israel. As you go, proclaim this message: 'The kingdom of heaven has come near.' "Do not get any gold or silver or copper to take with you in your belts— no bag for the journey, extra shirt or sandals or a staff, for the worker is worth his keep.

Whatever town or village you enter, search for a worthy person and stay at their house until you leave. As you enter the home, give it your greeting. If the home is deserving, let your peace rest on it; if not, let your peace return to you. If anyone will not welcome you or listen to your words, leave that home or town and shake the dust off your feet. Truly, it will be more bearable for Sodom and Gomorrah on the day of judgment than for that town.

"I am sending you out like sheep among wolves. Therefore, be as shrewd as snakes and as innocent as doves.

Be on your guard; you will be handed over to the local councils and be flogged in the synagogues. On my account, you will be brought before governors and kings as witnesses to them and the Gentiles. But when they arrest you, do not worry about what or how to say it. You will be given what to say at that time, for it will not be you speaking, but the Spirit of your Father speaking through you.

"Brother will betray brother to death, and a father his child; children will rebel against their parents and have them put to death. Everyone will hate you because of me, but the one who stands firm to the end will be saved. When you are persecuted in one place, flee to another. Truly, I tell you, you will not finish going through the towns of Israel before the Son of Man comes.

"The student is not above the teacher, nor a servant above his master. It is enough for students to be like their teachers and servants like their masters. If the head of the house has been called Beelzebul, how much more the members of his household! "So do not be afraid of them, for there is nothing concealed that will not be disclosed or hidden that will not be made known.

Do not be afraid of those who kill the body but cannot kill the soul. Instead, be afraid of the One who can destroy both soul and body in hell. Are not two sparrows sold for a penny? Yet not one of them will fall to the ground outside your Father's care. And even the very hairs of your head are all numbered. "Whoever acknowledges me before others, I will also acknowledge before my Father in heaven.

"Do not suppose I have come to bring peace to the

earth. I did not come to bring peace but a sword. For I have come to turn " ' a man against his father, a daughter against her mother, a daughter-in-law against her mother-in-law—a man's enemies will be the members of his own household.'

"Anyone who loves their father or mother more than me is not worthy of me; anyone who loves their son or daughter more than me is not worthy of me. Whoever does not take up their cross and follow me is not worthy of me. Whoever finds their life will lose it, and whoever loses their life for my sake will find it. "Anyone who welcomes you welcomes me, and anyone who welcomes me welcomes the one who sent me.

Whoever welcomes a prophet as a prophet will receive a prophet's reward, and whoever welcomes a righteous person as a righteous person will receive a righteous person's reward. And if anyone gives even a cup of cold water to one of these little ones who is my disciple, truly I tell you, that person will certainly not lose their reward." **(Matthew 10:1-7, 9-26, 28-30, 32, 34-42)**

Jesus turned this world upside down with 12 men who knew nothing about ministry, and one of them was a devil. Don't be shocked by the devil in your church. They are supposed to be there as a witness on the day of judgment of how merciful God is, even to give the devil a chance to follow God and REPENT, but he wouldn't, couldn't, maybe shouldn't, but is there for the ride, the money, glory, and fame. Wanting to shine is costly! Don't let your devil hinder your destiny. When it's time to let them go...let them go!

"Then Jesus replied, "Have I not chosen you, the Twelve? Yet one of you is a devil!" (He meant Judas, the son of Simon Iscariot, who, though one of the Twelve, was later to betray him.)"
(John 6:70-71)

"As soon as Judas took the bread, Satan entered into him. So Jesus told him, "What you are about to do, do quickly.""
(John 13:27)

Your Judas reminds you that the devil is close to you, not far away. Don't be afraid! That devil is close enough to you to kiss you but hates you and will sell you out in a heartbeat for money! They study you, know you, testify against you and convince sinners that you are sinners in hopes of destroying you. Don't REST, but RISE! We have Resurrected Power! Keep it moving…

Stay focused! Judas will catapult you to your highest calling if you quit and or give him too much credit for being unified with Satan to destroy your purpose. He may get you hung, but he will hang himself with no possible way of coming back. He went to church after he betrayed Jesus and got paid (most think God is blessing them for setting you up). Don't give too much attention to your Judas; it's just a matter of **TIME!** **SO praise God, not your troubles caused by your betrayer, who the devil used. " What you must do…do it quickly!" Let's get it over with…I have work to do after my crucifixion!**

The unbelievers constantly asked Jesus for a sign; Jesus said, "You will get no sign except for judgment." After all that Jesus had done, they still wanted to see signs.

Wanting a performance…for what?

We are often so busy looking for signs and the coming of Jesus in the heavens that we miss them right down here on earth. Our brothers and sisters who are in need, the great end-time harvest. In the flesh (carnal), we see many poor people with needs and problems, but in the spirit realm, God sees His children and plenty of resources to care for them. A great harvest ready to be picked and saved.

For I was hungry, and you gave me food: I was thirsty, and you gave me drink: I was a stranger, and you took me in: Naked, and you clothed me: I was sick, and you visited me: I was in prison, and you came unto me. Then shall the righteous answer him, saying, Lord, when saw we you hungry, and fed you? or thirsty, and gave you drink? When saw we you a stranger, and took you in? Or naked and clothed you? Or when saw we you sick, or in prison, and came unto you?

*And the King shall answer and say unto them, Verily I say unto you, Since you have done it unto one of the least of these my brethren, you have done it unto me. **(Mathew 25:35-40)***

Follow Jesus!

Do you know Lucifer, the fallen one, copies everything that God touches? He's like the great counterfeit of what's real. The devil has no power or authority to give you a life outside of this world. Everything he's bartering with is stolen. He has deceived so many.

Do you know that God chose "repentance" as our way out? It is the equalizer. All who do it get God's ear. John started a moment directed by God. Repentance is the way to God's heart. If we repent, God forgives our sins, and we get a clean slate. It doesn't matter what you've done. This is an act of Love and Mercy.

Salvation was a plan…a divine plan. God worked out all the kinks. The devil and his children would rather argue the facts than walk by faith and do what God says. John said, "REPENT." Jesus came after John and preached, " REPENT." The kingdom of heaven is now within your reach. God came to us because we were too sinful to go to Him.

Jesus openly said, "Follow Me." Think about our generation; social media asks people to follow them, "Follow me." We must challenge ourselves after "chapter BC and AD" to this man called Jesus getting his ministry going without marketing and technology…just word of mouth…"Follow Me." He got two followers at a time. His ministry EXPLODED! It was like nothing had ever been done or seen before. He called twelve to follow him and taught them, on the job, as they went.

Jesus did "On-the-job training." If Jesus turned the world upside down with "Follow Me" as the method and vehicle for his movement. This method was so unique and strategically put together that when the church was under persecution, they could go from house to house to have service, worship, and bible study teaching, hiding from their enemies. They couldn't worship as we do today and advertise; they had too many enemies and still grew expeditiously.

Jesus taught his disciples how to be effective and powerful in growth through "Social" without the "media" but the start of a new movement and way to real people. They invited them to follow (in person or by sending messages), friend request them, tag them, and even block those who felt they would threaten the movement. They were very discreet at times when it was necessary.

What was first has been made last and then first again. You don't think that in the end times, God would use what built the "First Church" to grow the "Last Church?" But this time, Satan had time to study the movement, plan, and technology. The copycat and counterfeit are on it! Everything God does, the baby wants it, too.

So Satan plans to use everything to get his campaign moving. He's the Anti-Christ, and he's sharpening his skills for this race. He's on a mission to be a thorn in the church's side. Be careful as to who you are following and who's following you. Where are you being led and leading others to? Imagine that day God pulled all our social media accounts as evidence for judgment. Are you ok with that? Would it be a problem?

The Beast is searching for his woman and his method! 666 is all around us. In trying times, he's marketing his destruction camouflaged with beauty, excitement, and feel-goods. One of the things prophesied was that people would be tired of all of the chaos and trouble and would become desperate for peace and safety because of fear.

"The dragon stood on the shore of the sea. And I saw a beast coming out of the sea. It had ten horns and seven heads, with ten crowns on its horns and on each head a blasphemous name. The beast I saw resembled a leopard but had feet like those of a bear and a mouth like that of a lion.

The dragon gave the beast his power and his throne and great authority. One of the heads of the beast seemed to have had a fatal wound, but the fatal wound had been healed. ***The whole world was filled with wonder and followed the beast.*** *People worshiped the dragon because he had given authority to the beast, and they also worshiped the beast and asked,* ***"Who is like the beast?*** *Who can wage war against it?"*

*The beast was given a mouth to utter proud words and blasphemies and to exercise its authority for **forty-two months**. It opened its mouth to blaspheme God and to slander his name and his dwelling place and those who live in heaven. It was given the power to wage war against God's holy people and to conquer them.* ***And it was given authority over every tribe, people, language, and nation.***

All inhabitants of the earth will worship the beast —all whose names have not been written in the Lamb's book of life, the Lamb who was slain from the world's creation. *Whoever has ears, let them hear. Because of the signs it was given the power to perform on behalf of the first beast, it deceived the inhabitants of the earth. It ordered them to set up an image in honor of the beast who was wounded by the sword and yet lived.*

The second beast was given the power to give breath to the image of the first beast so that the image could speak and cause all who refused to worship the image to be killed. It also forced all people, great and small, rich and poor, free and slave, to receive a mark on their right hands or their foreheads **so that they could not buy or sell unless they had the mark, which is the name of the beast or the number of its name. This calls for wisdom. Let the person with insight calculate the number of the beast, for it is the number of a man. That number is 666."** *(Revelation 13:1-9, 14-18)*

How powerful is this? John, the disciple turned apostle, is said to have been around 88 years old at the time of these writings. He's on an island, and Jesus appears to him and tells John to write what he sees. Jesus is revealing to him futuristic events. On this account, it does not make sense to John that he's seeing the future and trying to describe what he sees.

Remember when *"Jesus said this to indicate the kind of death by which Peter would glorify God. Then he said to him,* **"Follow me!"** *Peter turned and saw that the disciple whom Jesus loved was following them. (This was the one who had leaned back against Jesus at the supper and had said, "Lord, who is going to betray you?")*

When Peter saw him, he asked, "Lord, what about him?" Jesus answered, "If I want him to remain alive until I return, what is that to you? **You must follow me."** *Because of this, the rumor spread among the believers that this disciple would not die. But Jesus did not say that he would* *not die; he only said, "If I want him to remain alive until I return, what is that to you?"*

*This is the disciple who testifies to these things and who wrote them down. We know that his testimony is true. Jesus did many other things as well. If every one of them were written down, I suppose that even the whole world would not have room for the books that would be written." **(John 21:19-25)***

*"Then said Jesus unto his disciples, If any man will come after me, let him deny himself, take up his cross, and **follow me.** Whosoever will save his life shall lose it, and whosoever will lose his life for my sake shall find it. For what does a man profit if he shall gain the whole world and lose his own soul?*

*Or what shall a man give in exchange for his soul? For the Son of man shall come in the glory of his Father with his angels, and then he shall reward every man according to his works. Verily I say unto you, There be some standing here, which shall not taste of death, till they see the Son of man coming in his kingdom."(**Matthew 16:24-28 KJV**)*

"Until I return," this man saw Jesus, the last one standing there that day as a witness to this account. But what's more impressive to me is that John loved Jesus so much and was the youngest disciple of the twelve. By seeking God, loving God, and spending time devoted to God, he revealed many of heaven's secrets to John.

So young people, don't let anyone deter you from seeking God; he is not a bore. Don't let anyone tell you that you can't visit God or have heavenly experiences before you go there…or should I say, go home.

Be sure to know who you are **following** and what you are following. Be accountable because one day, you will be asked to give an account for the gifts you were given in life. **GREAT IS YOUR REWARD!**

Be sure to lead people to the light and life. **"Only follow me if I am following Christ!"**

Jesus is the originator of "FOLLOW ME."

CHAPTER FOUR
Passover

"Nothing but the BLOOD!"

"I Know It Was The Blood That Saved Me"

Passover, or Pesach in Hebrew, is one of the Jewish religion's most sacred and widely observed holidays. In Judaism, Passover commemorates the story of the Israelites' departure from ancient Egypt, which appears in the Hebrew Bible's books of Exodus, Numbers, and Deuteronomy, among other texts. Jews observe the week-long festival with several important rituals, including a traditional Passover meal known as a seder, removing leavened products from their home, substituting matzo for bread, and retelling the exodus.

According to the Hebrew Bible, Jewish settlement in ancient Egypt first occurred when Joseph, a son of the patriarch Jacob and founder of one of the 12 tribes of Israel, moved his family there during a severe famine in their homeland of Canaan. For many years, the Israelites lived in harmony in the province of Goshen, but the Egyptians began to see them as a threat as their population grew. After the death of Joseph and his brothers, the story goes, a particularly hostile pharaoh orders their enslavement and the systematic drowning of their firstborn sons in the Nile.

One of these doomed infants is rescued by the pharaoh's daughter, given the name Moses (meaning "one who is pulled out"), and adopted into the Egyptian royal family.

When he reaches adulthood, Moses becomes aware of his true identity and the Egyptians' brutal treatment of his fellow Hebrews. He kills an Egyptian slave master and escapes to the Sinai Peninsula, where he lives as a humble shepherd for forty years. One day, however, Moses received a command from God to return to Egypt and free his kin from bondage, according to the Hebrew Bible. Along with his brother Aaron, Moses approaches the reigning pharaoh (unnamed in the biblical version) several times, explaining that the Hebrew God has requested a three-day leave for his people to celebrate a feast in the wilderness.

When the pharaoh refuses, God unleashes ten plagues on the Egyptians, including turning the Nile River red with blood, diseased livestock, boils, hailstorms, and three days of darkness, culminating in the slaying of every firstborn son by an avenging angel. The Israelites, however, mark the door frames of their homes with lamb's blood so that the angel of death will recognize and "pass over" each Jewish household. Terrified of further punishment, the Egyptians convinced their ruler to release the Israelites, and Moses quickly led them out of Egypt. However, the pharaoh changes his mind and sends his soldiers to retrieve the former slaves.

As the Egyptian army approaches the fleeing Jews at the edge of the Red Sea, a miracle occurs: God causes the sea to part, allowing Moses and his followers to cross safely, then closes the passage and drowns the Egyptians. According to the Hebrew Bible, the Jews—now numbering in the hundreds of thousands—then trek through the Sinai desert for 40 tumultuous years before finally reaching their ancestral home in Canaan, later known as the Land of Israel.

One of the most important Passover rituals for observant Jews is removing all leavened food products (known as Chametz) from their home before the holiday begins and abstaining from them throughout its duration. Instead of bread, religious Jews eat a type of flatbread called matzo. According to tradition, this is because the Hebrews fled Egypt in such haste that there was no time for their bread to rise.

Passover also distinguishes itself from other Jewish holidays because it's primarily celebrated at home rather than at synagogue. This can make the holiday feel more like Thanksgiving than a traditional dress-up-and-go-to-services holiday. It also means that individual families have a lot of leeway to create and maintain their Passover traditions. It's doubtful that any two Seders you go to will be identical. Judaism is a religion of remembering, and the tradition of Passover is an excellent example of how the concept of memory preservation works in Judaism. The story of Passover includes multiple occasions when God protected the Hebrews because he remembered the promise he had made to them. Then, Passover is when Jews remember that God remembered them.

Why was Jesus in Jerusalem? Scriptures shared by Jews and Christians demand that three times a year, the faithful are to celebrate festivals in Jerusalem **(Exodus 23:14;**

2Chronicles 8:13); they are the feasts of Passover (Unleavened Bread), Weeks (Shavuot), and Booths (Tabernacles or Sukkot). The three are the appointed feasts listed in **Leviticus 23:2 (compare 2 Chronicles 31:3; Ezra 3:5).** Jerusalem, Zion, is the city of the feasts, as noted in **Isaiah 33:20.** The most important festival was Passover. Jesus was devoutly Jewish. According to **Luke (2:41–42),** Jesus's family went to Jerusalem yearly at Passover. When Jesus was 12, his parents went to the Temple, perhaps for his Bar Mitzvah (conceivably, his cousin, John, was present). According to sacred traditions, God demanded that all males appear in Jerusalem to celebrate Passover **(Exodus 23:17; Deuteronomy 16:16).** All must recline to dine, a straightforward arrangement in Jesus's Last Supper according to **John 13:23.**

According to **Mark (14:12–21), Matthew (26:17–25), Luke (22:7–14, 21–23),** and **John (13:21–30),** Jesus was in Jerusalem to celebrate Passover. The first three gospels described the first day of Passover when approximately 10,000 lambs were slaughtered in the Temple; Jesus's disciples prepared the Passover meal in the upper room of a house in southwest Jerusalem. Jesus's last supper was either the Passover meal (according to Matthew, Mark, and Luke) or just before Passover, with Passover traditions informing the evening (John). Following customs that are now well over 2,000 years old, Jesus broke bread, raised a cup full of wine, and chanted the Passover hymn. If Jesus broke "leavened bread," it was not matzah, and it could not be a Passover meal. **Mark (14:26)** adds, "When they had sung the hymn, they went out to the Mount of Olives."

Why was that Week important? The annual pilgrimage

to Jerusalem is the time in the Spring when Jews celebrate God's formation of Israel when he delivered the nation from slavery in Egypt. The yearly celebration is shaped by a shared memory of that deliverance and a focus on experiencing a new God's pivotal miracle. Passover continued for seven days (Exodus 12:15; Leviticus 23:6), beginning on the fourteenth of the first month in the evening. The paschal lamb was eaten on the first evening **(Exodus 12:6, 8).**

Long before Jesus, Jewish traditions reflected a long, sacred commemoration of Passover each year. For example, those with Moses left the city of Rameses in Egypt the day after the initial Passover. According to **Joshua (5:10),** Israelites celebrated Passover at Gilgal, while King Josiah celebrated the Passover in Jerusalem (2 Chronicles 35:1,16). And those returning from the Babylonian exile celebrated the Passover (Ezra 6:19). Knowing these ancient traditions helps us appreciate Jesus's wish: "I have eagerly desired to eat this Passover with you" **(Luke 22:15).**

The traditions in the Passover Haggadah (literally "The Telling of the Passover Story") antedate Jesus. It is a "scroll" or book that Jews read on the first night of Passover to commemorate "the Season of our freedom in love, a holy convocation, commemorating the departure from Egypt." As the wine cup is raised, Jews bless "the LORD, our God, King of the universe."

Within a few decades of Jesus's Passover, Paul coined the concept that "Christ our paschal lamb has been sacrificed." He urged Jesus's followers to continue to celebrate Passover: "Let us celebrate the feast, (but) not with the old leaven of malice and evil" **(1 Corinthians 5:7–8).**

Paul seems to know the Passover Haggadah. First, in 1 Corinthians 10:4, Paul implies that the rock followed after the Hebrews in their wanderings; according to the Passover Haggadah, the rock was round. It rolled itself up like a swarm of bees and followed the Hebrews. Paul helps with a symbolic meaning by adding that it is "the spiritual rock that followed them." Second, in 1 Corinthians 10:16, in the celebration of Passover, Paul mentions "the cup of blessing;" the leader says those exact words of the seder.

Thus, Jesus's Last Supper becomes "the Lord's Supper," the Eucharist. Fluid traditions swirled in the minds of Jesus's first followers as the Exodus from Egypt framed the life and departure of Jesus. Today, Jews celebrate Passover (in Jesus's language); many look for the coming of the Messiah. Christians celebrate Passover as Easter. Many remember that the Messiah has come and memorized words like these (in over one hundred languages): "On the evening of Jesus's last supper, he took bread. Giving thanks, he said this is my body, as you eat it, remember me. After supper, Jesus took a chalice and said, drink this wine in memory of me."

In Jerusalem today, Jews and Christians gather around a table with their respective families and celebrate an ancient festival: breaking bread and drinking wine. Memory flavors life with meaning; two groups remember God's mighty Salvific works, with words pregnant with a kaleidoscope of meanings: "And out of Egypt I called my son" **(Hosea 11:1).**

A household member chooses a one-year-old unblemished male lamb for the Passover. (In A. D. 33, Nisan 10 fell on 'Palm Monday,' the day Jesus made his triumphal entry into Jerusalem. On that day, he presented himself as the unblemished sacrifice for the nation.) The slaughter of the lambs would not take place until Nisan 14, the day Jesus was crucified **(Friday, April 3, A. D. 33).**

Usually, the evening before the Passover meal was eaten, the *paterfamilias* led his family through the house by candlelight, looking in nooks and crannies for any leaven in the house. No leaven was supposed to be in the home at that time. (Not infrequently, Jews would sell their leaven to their Gentile neighbors and repurchase it after the eight days of unleavened bread!)

As guests and family members entered the home to celebrate Passover, a servant or slave would often be there to wash their feet. This was the task of the lowest class of people. (Jesus did this in (John 13), even though he was the paterfamilias or head of the family; both symbolize what he would later do for his disciples [**cf. Mark 10:45**—"The Son of man did not come to be served, but to serve, and to give my life as a ransom for many"] and embodies his principle that "If anyone wants to be first, he shall be last of all, and servant of all" [**Mark 9:35; cf. also John 13:15**].)
"Blessed are you, O Lord our God, king of the universe, who has created the fruit of the vine…"

"Blessed are you, O Lord our God, King of the Universe who brings forth bread from the earth. Blessed are you, O Lord our God, King of the universe, who has sanctified us with your commandments and commanded us to eat unleavened bread."

The host breaks the guest of honor's bread and dips it together in the Charoseth and bitter herbs. The guest, in turn, breaks his neighbor's bread and dips it together, and so on down the line.

"The name of the Lord be blessed from now until eternity. Let us bless him of whose gifts we have partaken: Blessed be our God of whose gifts we have partaken, and by whose goodness we exist."

"Blessed are you, O Lord our God, king of the universe, who has created the fruit of the vine. . .

"**I will redeem** you with an outstretched arm and great judgments."

"Then **I will take** you as my people, and I will be your God, and you shall know that I am the Lord Your God who brought you out from under the burdens of the Egyptians."

Passover lambs were slain between noon and 3 p.m., and there were three hours of darkness, from noon to 3 p.m., when Jesus was on the cross [Mark 15:33]. When Jesus died, the temple curtain was torn in two, from top to bottom **[Mark 15:38]**—right when the last lambs would be on the altar in front of the sanctuary!). In A. D. 70, the previous year that the temple was still standing, 270,000 lambs were slain.

When the lambs were slain, the Levites repeatedly chanted the Psalms (Psalms 113-118).

This practice stems from a rabbinic interpretation of **Zephaniah 1:12**—"I will search Jerusalem with lamps and punish those who are complacent.'" Since leaven often represents sin, Paul makes the tie between the leaven of the Passover and our commitment to Christ in 1 Cor. 5:7 ("Get rid of the old leaven that you may be a new batch without leaven—as you are. For Christ, our Passover lamb, has been sacrificed.")

Jesus was that Passover Lamb and still is, The Lamb of God who take away the sins of the world.

I asked a friend of mine who is a Jew (Israelite), "Do you accept Jesus as the Messiah, the Passover Lamb prophesied to come?" He said, "No way!" I asked, " Why Not?" "Because the Messiah has not come yet," he said. I asked, "What evidence do you have to support that theory?" He responded, "According to the Law of Moses."

So I asked, "Do you guys still bring your lambs without marks or blemish for the atonement for you and your family's sins for the year?" "No, he said." Then I asked, "Why not? If Jesus is not the Messiah, Son of God and Lamb of God, sent by God to fulfill prophecy, then who was he? ...And why are you guys not bring you lams or sheep to the Passover to be sacrificed for the atonement of your sins as a people?"

This is the Law of Moses, which is still in effect. " HE said he would ask his priest and get back to me. Well, he did it very timely, and I was impressed. Excited, I was very eager to hear the answer. I might have missed something because I'm not Jewish. My friend said, "His priest would get back to him after he reached out to someone in Israel." Long story short, they had no answer for me, in my case… **Jesus is the Answer**.

According to the Levitical Law, each family or household was required to sacrifice sheep or goats for the atonement of their sins. The animal was slayed as the living sacrifice (altar), and blood was put in a bowl for the person or family. At Passover, the requirement was to bring your very best offering (lamb/sheep) without spot or blemish— perfect.

Your offering is taken behind the veil, slayed, pouring the blood into a bowl, and then brought out to perform the ritual or tradition of the sins being removed from the person and persons to whom the sacrifice was presented. This atonement for the sins committed was beloved to have been removed and covered until the following Passover, which would be for a year. Passover is a seven-day (Holy Week) celebration and service to the people.

Jesus was at Passover week and is noted for his triumphal entry into Jerusalem on a donkey. This is widely seen as a recapitulation of the enthronement of Solomon (described in 1 Kings: 1), where at King David's direction, he is anointed as king *at the Gihon Spring and rides his father's donkey into the city to the acclaim of the people. When Jesus rode into Jerusalem on a donkey,* the Jews knew what it meant. They shouted out, "Hosanna, Hosanna!

"On the next day, many people that were come to the feast, when they heard that Jesus was coming to Jerusalem,

took branches of palm trees and went forth to meet him, and cried, Hosanna: Blessed is the King of Israel that cometh in the name of the Lord. And Jesus, when he had found a young ass, sat thereon; as it is written, Fear not, daughter of Sion: behold, thy King cometh, sitting on an ass's colt. These things understood not his disciples at first: but when Jesus was glorified, then remembered they that these things were written of him and that they had done these things unto him. The people, therefore, that were with him when he called Lazarus out of his grave and raised him from the dead, bare record.

*For this cause, the people also met him; they heard that he had done this miracle. The Pharisees, therefore, said among themselves, Perceive ye how ye prevail nothing? Behold, the world is gone after him." **John 12:12-19 KJV***

King David wanted to establish his favored son Solomon as his successor when he was ancient. So he arranged for Solomon to ride on David's mule in the company of Zadok, the priest, and Nathan, the prophet. By entering the city on a donkey, Jesus was proclaimed king by the Pharisees and priests (Jesus is noted as a prophet, Priest, and King). They couldn't see that, and neither were they trying to. Jesus was from Nazareth, which was enough to fuel the fire of the Pharisees (Tribe of Levy); they were the elite group (Levites) of all the tribes of Israel… prosperous and dignified.

Jesus is also referred to as The Son of David, *"The book of the generation of Jesus Christ, the son of David, the son of Abraham (Mathew 1:1), And all the people were amazed, and said, Is this not the son of David (Mathew*

*12:23), While the Pharisees were gathered together, Jesus asked them, Saying, What think you of Christ? Whose son is he? They say to him, The son of David **(Mathew 22:41,42),***

*And, behold, two blind men sitting by the wayside, when they heard that Jesus passed by, cried out, saying, Have mercy on us, O, Lord, you son of David. And the multitude rebuked them because they should hold their peace: but they cried the more, saying, Have mercy on us, O, Lord, you son of David. And Jesus stood still, and called them, and said, What will you that I shall do to you? They say to him, Lord, that our eyes may be opened. So Jesus had compassion on them, and touched their eyes: and immediately their eyes received sight, and they followed him **(Mathew 20:30-34)**.*

*Many people of the Jews, therefore, knew that he was there, and they came not for Jesus' sake only but that they might see Lazarus also, whom he had raised from the dead. But the chief priests consulted that they might put Lazarus also to death; Because that by reason of him, many of the Jews went away and believed in Jesus. On the next day, many people that came to the feast, when they heard that Jesus was coming to Jerusalem, Took branches of palm trees, **went forth to meet him, and cried, Hosanna: Blessed is the King of Israel that comes in the name of the Lord. This is where we get "Palm Sunday."***

And Jesus, when he had found a young ass, sat thereon; as it is written, Fear not, daughter of Sion: behold, your King comes, sitting on an ass's colt. These things understood not his disciples at first: but when Jesus was glorified, then remembered they that these things were *written of him and that they had done these things to him. The people, therefore, were with him when he called Lazarus out of his grave and raised him from the dead bore record. For this cause, the people also met him, and they heard that he had done this miracle. The Pharisees, therefore, said among themselves, Perceive you how you prevail nothing? Behold, the world is gone after him. **(John 12:9-19)(KJV)***

On the first day of the feast of unleavened bread, the disciples came to Jesus, saying, Where wilt thou that we prepare for thee to eat the Passover? And he said, Go into the city to such a man, and say unto him, The Master saith, My time is at hand; I will keep the Passover at thy house with my disciples. The disciples did as Jesus had appointed them, and they made the Passover ready.

When the event came, he sat down with the twelve of them. And as they did eat, he said, Verily I say unto you, that one of you shall betray me. And they were exceeding sorrowful, and began every one of them to say unto him, Lord, is it I? And he answered and said, He that dips his hand with me in the dish, the same shall betray me. The Son of man goeth as it is written of him: but woe unto that man by whom the Son of man is betrayed! It would have been good for that man if he had not been born. Then Judas, who betrayed him, answered and said, Master, is it I?

He said unto him, Thou hast said, and as they were eating, Jesus took bread, blessed it, brake it, gave it to the disciples, and said, Take, eat; this is my body. And he took the cup, and gave thanks, and gave it to them, saying, Drink ye all of it; For this is my blood of the new testament, which is shed for many for the remission of sins. But I say unto you. I will not drink henceforth of this fruit of the vine until that day when I drink it new with you in my Father's kingdom.

After singing a hymn, they went out into the Mount of Olives. Then saith Jesus unto them, All ye shall be offended because of me this night: for it is written, I will smite the shepherd, and the sheep of the flock shall be scattered abroad. But after I am risen again, I will go before you into Galilee.
(Mathew 26:17-32)

Jesus broke himself at that Passover Feast as the Lamb of God, which is why his legs couldn't be broken at the cross. For these things were done, the scripture should be fulfilled: *"A bone of him shall not be broken. And again another scripture saith, They shall look on him whom they pierced.*
(John 19:36-37)

Jesus established the new "Kingdom Order" and standard for Passover. To this day, Passover is celebrated and observed globally, and wine and bread are used; there is no other form of lamb or blood sacrifice. Why do we fight the truth of God? If Jesus (Yeshua, Messiah) is not the Lamb of God…then who is?

The next day, John sees Jesus coming unto him and saith, Behold the Lamb of God, which taketh away the sin of the world. This is he of whom I said, After me cometh a man which is preferred before me: for he was before me. And I knew him not: but that he should be made manifest to Israel, therefore am I come baptizing with water. And John bare record, saying, I saw the Spirit descending from heaven like a dove, and it abode upon him.

And I knew him not: but he that sent me to baptize with water, the same said unto me, Upon whom thou shalt see the Spirit descending, and remaining on him, the same is he which baptizes with the Holy Ghost. And I saw, and bare record, that this is the Son of God.

Again the next day after John stood, and two of his disciples; And looking upon Jesus as he walked, he saith, Behold the Lamb of God! (John 1:29-36)

And I saw in his right hand that sat on the throne a book written within and on the backside, sealed with seven seals. And I saw a strong angel proclaiming with a loud voice, Who is worthy to open the book, and to lose the seals thereof? And no man in heaven, nor earth, neither under the earth, was able to open the book, neither to look thereon.

And I wept much because no man was found worthy to open and to read the book, neither to look thereon. And one of the elders saith unto me, Weep not: behold, the Lion of the tribe of Juda, the Root of David, hath prevailed to open the book, and to loose the seven seals thereof. And I beheld, and, lo, in the midst of the throne and of the four beasts, and in the midst of the elders, stood a Lamb as it had been slain, having seven horns and seven eyes, which are the seven Spirits of God sent forth into all the earth. And he came and took the book out of his right hand that sat upon the throne.

And when he had taken the book, the four beasts and four and twenty elders fell down before the Lamb, having every one of them harps and golden vials full of odors, which are the prayers of saints. And they sung a new song, saying, Thou art worthy to take the book, and to open the seals thereof: for thou wast slain, and hast redeemed us to God by thy blood out of every kindred, and tongue, and people, and nation; And hast made us unto our God kings and priests: and we shall reign on the earth.

And I beheld, and I heard the voice of many angels round about the throne and the beasts and the elders: and the number of them was ten thousand times ten thousand, and thousands of thousands; Saying with a loud voice, Worthy is the Lamb that was slain to receive power, and riches, and wisdom, and strength, and honor, and glory, and blessing.

And every creature which is in heaven, and on the earth, and under the earth, and such as are in the sea, and all that are in them, heard I saying, Blessing, and honor, and glory, and power, be unto him that sits upon the throne, and unto the Lamb forever and ever.
And the four beasts said, Amen. And the four and twenty elders fell down and worshipped him that liveth forever and ever. **(Revelation Chapter 5)**

All the evidence points to Jesus as the fulfillment of the Old Testament prophesies (types and shadows of what's to come—the **real**). He is the Passover! He is the Lamb of God! He is the Son of God; he was and is the last needed sacrifice and the burnt offering, accepted by God! The religious leaders burned him, betrayed him, hated him, killed him, and tried to eradicate him, but you cannot get rid of God either in time or eternity. Lucifer-Satan-the, the

Devil, has already tried, on many attempts. This is why his death was so barbaric and brutal; it was a ***"Hate Crime!"***

The Blood of Christ

"But when Christ came as high priest of the good things that are now already here, he went through the greater and more perfect tabernacle that is not made with human hands, that is to say, is not a part of this creation. He did not enter by means of the blood of goats and calves, but he entered the Most Holy Place once for all by his own blood, thus obtaining eternal redemption. The blood of goats and bulls and the ashes of a heifer sprinkled on those who are ceremonially unclean sanctify them so that they are outwardly clean. How much more, then, will the blood of Christ, who through the eternal Spirit offered himself unblemished to God, cleanse our consciences from acts that lead to death so that we may serve the living God! For this reason, Christ is the mediator of a new covenant, and those called may receive the promised eternal inheritance—now that he has died as a ransom to set them free from the sins committed under the first covenant. In the case of a will, it is necessary to prove the death of the one who made it. This is why even the first covenant was not put into effect without blood.

When Moses proclaimed every command of the law to all the people, he took the blood of calves, water, scarlet wool, and branches of hyssop and sprinkled the scroll and all the people. He said, "This is the blood of the covenant, which God has commanded you to keep." In the same way, he sprinkled the tabernacle with blood and everything used in its ceremonies. In fact, the law requires that nearly everything be cleansed with blood, and without the shedding of blood, there is no forgiveness.

It was then necessary for the copies of the heavenly things to be purified with these sacrifices, but the heavenly things themselves had better sacrifices than these. Christ did not enter a sanctuary made with human hands that was only a copy of the true one; he entered heaven itself, now to appear for us in God's presence. Nor did he enter heaven to offer himself again and again, the way the high priest enters the Most Holy Place every year with blood that is not his own.

*Otherwise, Christ would have had to suffer many times since the creation of the world. But he has appeared once and for all at the culmination of the ages to do away with sin by sacrificing himself. Just as people are destined to die once and after that to face judgment, so Christ was sacrificed once to take away the sins of many, and he will appear a second time, not to bear sin, but to bring salvation to those waiting for him.***"Hebrews 9:11-16, 18-28 NIV**

They continued to offer up blood from sheep and lambs long after Jesus was crucified. Stubborn and religious were they....Where are they now?

Chapter Five
The Cross

Jesus Didn't Just Die For You But Died As You So You Can Become Him, As He Became You...

Jesus came and died as the second and last man, Adam, to give us our place back with God. We were reconciled and restored to our place in God. We must, in turn, receive what he's done and die according to the Adam concept. The curse has been nailed to the cross, and my blessed life came out of the grave with Jesus, who is now sitting in heavenly places, lifting me up beside him and calling me blessed! RISE UP, PEOPLE OF GOD...RISE UP!

As complex and challenging as it was, Jesus went to that cross! It wasn't easy at all. We see the decorated versions of the cross and, in some regards, miss the point of pain and sacrifice. Why would someone sacrifice their life and submit to such disgrace and shame?

"For God so loved the world, that he gave his only begotten Son, that whosoever believes in him should not perish, but have everlasting life. For God sent not his Son into the world to condemn the world; but that the world through him might be saved." (John 3:16-17 KJV)

The Suffering Servant,

* * *

"Who has believed our message, and to whom has the arm of the Lord been revealed? He grew up before him like a tender shoot and like a root out of dry ground. He had no beauty or majesty to attract us to him, and there was nothing in his appearance that we should desire him. He was despised and rejected by humanity, a man of suffering and familiar with pain. Like one from whom people hide their faces, he was despised, and we held him in low esteem.

Surely, he took up our pain and bore our suffering, yet we considered him punished by God, stricken by him, and afflicted. But he was pierced for our transgressions and crushed for our iniquities; the punishment that brought us peace was on him, and by his wounds, we are healed. We all, like sheep, have gone astray; each of us has turned to our way, and the Lord has laid on him the iniquity of us all. He was oppressed and afflicted, yet he did not open his mouth; he was led like a lamb to the slaughter, and as a sheep, before its shearers are silent, he did not open his mouth. By oppression and judgment, he was taken away. Yet, who of his generation protested? For he was cut off from the land of the living; for the transgression of my people, he was punished.

He was assigned a grave with the wicked and with the rich in his death, though he had done no violence, nor was there any deceit in his mouth. Yet it was the Lord's will to crush him and cause him to suffer, and though the Lord makes his life an offering for sin, he will see his offspring and prolong his days, and the will of the Lord will prosper in his hand.

* * *

*After he has suffered, he will see the light of life and be satisfied; by his knowledge, my righteous servant will justify many, and he will bear their iniquities. Therefore, I will give him a portion among the great, and he will divide the spoils with the strong because he poured out his life unto death and was numbered with the transgressors. For he bore the sin of many and made intercession for the transgressors." **Isaiah 53:1-12 NIv.**

The Cross

We are saved by what Jesus did at the cross, on the cross. No matter what the enemy thought he was doing, God was in control; the cross was his divine plan. His death was a reflection of how much Lucifer's hate for God. He was jealous...so jealous. Get this: it is thc first time the devil gets his hour to put his hands on God for the first time, without security or restrictions. The devil knew the angels were present but forbidden to make a move. Satan is not that powerful. God tied his own hands to give Satan confidence that nothing would happen to him, so express yourself. The brutality of the death of our Lord Jesus Christ was the enemy's very true heart expressed.

This enemy hates our God! God never died before, and now, what's going to happen? Satan putting his hands on God was the most incredible high he ever had, but like all drugs, they can't last forever, but his heart was put on public display. Now, the angels got to see the truth God had for them. Lucifer hated me even when he was here in the family. He didn't show it, like a person planning a murder. A lying, cheating spouse who thinks you don't know they are cheating. Lucifer thought he was getting away with his hypocrisy.

"Then he called the crowd to him along with his disciples and said: "Whoever wants to be my disciple must deny themselves and take up their cross and follow me." **(Mark 8:34 NIV)**

"For the message of the cross is foolishness to those who are perishing, but to us who are being saved it is the power of God." **(1 Corinthians 1:18 NIV)**

"For the message of the cross is foolishness to those who are perishing, but to us who are being saved, it is the power of God."
   1 Corinthians 1:18 NIV

The cross was brutal, bloody, evil, painful, and necessary, the very exact expression of the devil's hate for God. Love brought God to this world, and hate took him out!

It was the **cross** that God used to save us! It was the hardest thing God has ever done, according to records. We should not take lightly what he's done for us. How would anyone be able to stand before Jesus and ignore the pain and suffering?

"Therefore, since we are surrounded by such a great cloud of witnesses, let us throw off everything that hinders and the sin that so easily entangles. And let us run with perseverance the race marked out for us, fixing our eyes on Jesus, the pioneer and perfecter of faith. For the joy set before him, he endured the cross, scorning its shame, and

*sat down at the right hand of the throne of God. Consider him who endured such opposition from sinners so that you will not grow weary and lose heart." **(Hebrews 12:1-3 NIV)***

"But God demonstrates his own love for us in this: While we were still sinners, Christ died for us."
Romans 5:8 NIV.

Religion without the presence of God is lethal. It is so sad how people can dedicate their entire lives to a religion and not have a clue as to who God is. The Pharisees represented the elite and masters of the word of God in their time. No one was considered as influential and astute as the Pharisees and Sadducees. They knew God's word like the back of their hands, but even still, they did not know God as well as they thought.

They fought the will of God every step of the way to fulfill the prophecies. To the people, they were as close as you get to God until God showed up. This is an excellent place to observe and evaluate. Let's look at how far off the church leaders were and how they handled the same God in-home they taught and preached about every week. Sometimes, we can do something for so long that we don't even realize we've lost sight of why we do what we do... we're just doing it. What's the point, and better yet, what's the purpose?

These leaders had lost the whole reason why they were called to the priesthood in the first place. They could quote scripture but cannot live what they quoted. When Jesus showed up at twelve, they admired him and were impressed with his knowledge of God's word and wisdom. But, when he returned as a grown man, the same hated him. As a child, Jesus posed no threat, but as a grown man, his living example of God's word exposed the religious leaders' misappropriation of that same word, God's people, and alluded to the truth.

The amazing thing is that people whom God has anointed sometimes think they can stop the God in you if misguided by the wrong spirit. This is what happened to King Saul and David. Saul thought he could use his anointing to destroy God's newly anointed. This is not what your anointing is to be used for. The Pharisees were operating in the same spirit as Saul. They thought they could stop Jesus from doing what he was called to do. How can you use God against God? *"A kingdom divided against itself cannot stand."* Jesus would not allow religion to come in between his relationship with God. So, I want to encourage you to define your vision, know it came from God, and if so, no one can stop you because they cannot STOP God! Don't give power to anyone to separate you from your God! *"Me and my Father are one and the same."*

Religious Leaders part in leading to Jesus' arrest, trial, condemnation, and ultimately, his crucifixion.

Take a look at how Jesus rebukes the religious leaders for coming against the will of God, even when they think you are doing the will of God. If we do not humble ourselves, we can be on the wrong side of God while preaching and teaching the word of God. They were so misguided:

"Then some Pharisees and teachers of the law came to Jesus from Jerusalem and asked, "Why do your disciples break the tradition of the elders? They don't wash their hands before they eat!" Jesus replied, "And why do you break the command of God for the sake of your tradition? For God said, 'Honor your father and mother' and 'Anyone who curses their father or mother is to be put to death.'

But you say that if anyone declares that what might have been used to help their father or mother is 'devoted to God,' they are not to 'honor their father or mother' with it. Thus, you nullify the word of God for the sake of your tradition. You hypocrites! Isaiah was right when he prophesied about you:" 'These people honor me with their lips, but their hearts are far from me.

They worship me in vain; their teachings are merely human rules.' " Jesus called the crowd and said, "Listen and understand. What goes into someone's mouth does not defile them, but what comes out of their mouth, that is what defiles them." Then the disciples asked him, "Do you know that the Pharisees were offended when they heard this?" He replied, "Every plant my heavenly Father has not planted will be pulled up by the roots. Leave them; they are blind guides.

If the blind lead the blind, both will fall into a pit." Peter said, "Explain the parable to us." "Are you still so dull?" Jesus asked them. But the things that come out of a person's mouth come from the heart, and these defile them. For out of the heart come evil thoughts—murder, adultery, sexual immorality, theft, false testimony, slander. These are *what defile a person, but eating with unwashed hands does not defile them." **Matthew 15:1-16, 18-20 NIV***

*"Then the Pharisees went out and laid plans to trap him in his words. They sent their disciples to him along with the Herodians. "Teacher," they said, "we know that you are a man of integrity and that you teach the way of God in accordance with the truth. You aren't swayed by others because you pay no attention to who they are. Tell us then, what is your opinion? Is it right to pay the imperial tax to Caesar or not?" But Jesus, knowing their evil intent, said, "You hypocrites, why are you trying to trap me? Show me the coin used to pay the tax." They brought him a denarius, "Caesar's," they replied. Then he told them, "So give back to Caesar what is Caesar's, and to God what is God's." When they heard this, they were amazed. So they left him and went away." **Matthew 22:15-19, 21-22 NIV.***

A Warning Against Hypocrisy

"Then Jesus said to the crowds and his disciples: "The teachers of the law and the Pharisees sit in Moses' seat. So you must be careful to do everything they tell you. But do not do what they do, for they do not practice what they preach. They tie up heavy, cumbersome loads and put them on other people's shoulders, but they themselves are not willing to lift a finger to move them.

"Everything they do is done for people to see: They make their phylacteries wide and the tassels on their garments long; they love the place of honor at banquets and the most important seats in the synagogues; they love to be greeted with respect in the marketplaces and to be called

'Rabbi' by others. "But you are not to be called 'Rabbi,' for you have one Teacher and are all brothers.

*And do not call anyone on earth 'father,' for you have one Father, who is in heaven. Nor are you to be called instructors, for you have one Instructor, the Messiah. The greatest among you will be your servant. Those who exalt themselves will be humbled, and those who humble themselves will be exalted." **Matthew 23:1-12 NIV***

The Hypocrisy of the Sadducees

"That same day, the Sadducees, who say there is no resurrection, came to him with a question. "Teacher," they said, "Moses told us that if a man dies without having children, his brother must marry the widow and raise offspring for him. Now, there were seven brothers among us. The first one married and died, and since he had no children, he left his wife to his brother. The same thing happened to the second and third brother down to the seventh.

*Now, at the resurrection, whose wife will she be of the seven since all of them were married to her?" Jesus replied, "You are in error because you do not know the Scriptures or the power of God. At the resurrection, people will neither marry nor be given in marriage; they will be like the angels in heaven. But about the resurrection of the dead—have you not read what God said to you, 'I am the God of Abraham, the God of Isaac, and the God of Jacob'? He is not the God of the dead but of the living." When the crowds heard this, they were astonished at his teaching." **Matthew 22:23-26, 28-33 NIV***

Seven Woes on the Teachers of the Law and the Pharisees

"Woe to you, teachers of the law and Pharisees, you hypocrites! You shut the door of the kingdom of heaven in people's faces. You yourselves do not enter, nor will you let those enter who are trying to. "Woe to you, teachers of the law and Pharisees, you hypocrites! You travel over land and sea to win a single convert, and when you have succeeded, you make them twice as much a child of hell as you are.

"Woe to you, blind guides! You say, 'If anyone swears by the temple, it means nothing, but anyone who swears by the temple's gold is bound by that oath.' You blind fools! Which is greater: the gold or the temple that makes the gold sacred? You also say, 'If anyone swears by the altar, it means nothing, but anyone who swears by the gift on the altar is bound by that oath.' You blind men!

Which is greater: the gift or the altar that makes the gift sacred? Therefore, anyone who swears by the altar swears by it and by everything on it. And anyone who swears by the temple swears by it and by the one who dwells in it. And anyone who swears by heaven swears by God's throne and by the one who sits on it. "Woe to you, teachers of the law and Pharisees, you hypocrites!

You give a tenth of your spices—mint, dill, and cumin. But you have neglected the more important matters of the law—justice, mercy, and faithfulness. You should have practiced the latter without neglecting the former. You blind guides! You strain out a gnat but swallow a camel. "Woe to you, teachers of the law and Pharisees, you hypocrites! You clean the outside of the cup and dish, but inside, they are full of greed and self-indulgence. Blind Pharisee! First, clean the inside of the cup and dish, and then the outside also will be clean. "Woe to you, teachers of the law and Pharisees, you hypocrites!

You are like whitewashed tombs, which look beautiful on the outside but on the inside are full of the bones of the dead and everything unclean. In the same way, on the outside, you appear to people as righteous, but on the inside, you are full of hypocrisy and wickedness. "Woe to you, teachers of the law and Pharisees, you hypocrites! You build tombs for the prophets and decorate the graves of the righteous. And you say, 'If we had lived in the days of our ancestors, we would not have taken part with them in shedding the blood of the prophets.' So you testify against yourselves that you are the descendants of those who murdered the prophets. Go ahead, then, and complete what your ancestors started! "You Snakes! You brood of vipers! How will you escape being condemned to hell?

Therefore, I am sending you prophets, sages, and teachers. Some of them you will kill and crucify; others you will flog in your synagogues and pursue from town to town. And so upon you will come all the righteous blood that has been shed on earth, from the blood of righteous Abel to the blood of Zechariah, son of Berekiah, whom you murdered between the temple and the altar.

Truly, I tell you, all this will come on this generation. "Jerusalem, Jerusalem, you who kill the prophets and stone those sent to you, how often I have longed to gather your *children together, as a hen gathers her chicks under her wings, and you were not willing. Look, your house is left to you desolate. **For I tell you, you will not see me again until you say, 'Blessed is he who comes in the name of the Lord.'"** Matthew 23:13, 15-39 NIV*

Judas Agrees to Betray Jesus

*"Then one of the Twelve—the one called Judas Iscariot—went to the chief priests and asked, "What are you willing to give me if I deliver him over to you?" So they counted out for him thirty pieces of silver. From then on, Judas watched for an opportunity to hand him over." **Matthew 26:14-16 NIV***

"Offenses must come, but woe unto the person/persons who agreed with the devil to be used to offend you." Great is your reward, my brothers and sisters of the kingdom.

I know it hurts right now, but God knows your pain….Thank you, Jesus!

One day, you will walk up and feel the pain no more. Just watch and see. This, too, shall pass...

Don't worry when close ones betray you because Jesus is our example; keep your eyes on the prize.

My God! I feel the Holy Ghost's Fire!

"And it came to pass when Jesus had finished all these sayings, he said unto his disciples, Ye know that after two days is the feast of the Passover, and the Son of man is

betrayed to be crucified. Then, they assembled the chief priests, the scribes, and the elders of the people unto the palace of the high priest, who was called Caiaphas, and consulted that they might take Jesus by subtlety and kill him. But they said, Not on the feast day, lest there be an uproar among the people." **Matthew 26:1-5 KJV**

Gethsemane

"Then Jesus went with his disciples to a place called Gethsemane, and he said to them, "Sit here while I go over there and pray." He took Peter and the two sons of Zebedee along with him, and he began to be sorrowful and troubled. Then he said to them, "My soul is overwhelmed with sorrow to the point of death. Stay here and keep watch with me." Going a little farther, he fell with his face to the ground and prayed, "My Father, if it is possible, may this cup be taken from me.

Yet not as I will, but as you will." Then, he returned to his disciples and found them sleeping. "Couldn't you men keep watch with me for one hour?" he asked Peter. "Watch and pray so that you will not fall into temptation. The spirit is willing, but the flesh is weak." He went away a second time and prayed, "My Father if it is not possible for this cup to be taken away unless I drink it, may your will be done." When he came back, he again found them sleeping because their eyes were heavy.

Then he returned to the disciples and asked them, "Are you still sleeping and resting? Look, the hour has come, and the Son of Man is delivered into the hands of sinners. Rise! Let us go! Here comes my betrayer!"

Matthew 26:36-43, 45-46 NIV

Jesus Arrested

"While he was still speaking, Judas, one of the Twelve, arrived. With him was a large crowd armed with swords and clubs sent from the chief priests and the elders of the people. Now, the betrayer had arranged a signal with them: "The one I kiss is the man; arrest him." Going at once to Jesus, Judas said, "Greetings, Rabbi!" and kissed him. Jesus replied, "Do what you came for, friend."

Then, the men stepped forward, seized Jesus, and arrested him. With that, one of Jesus' companions reached for his sword, drew it out, and struck the servant of the high priest, cutting off his ear. "Put your sword back in its place," Jesus said to him, "for all who draw the sword will die by the sword. But how then would the Scriptures be fulfilled that say it must happen in this way?"

In that hour, Jesus said to the crowd, "Am I leading a rebellion that you have come out with swords and clubs to capture me? Every day, I sat in the temple courts teaching, and you did not arrest me. But this has all taken place that the writings of the prophets might be fulfilled." Then all the disciples deserted him and fled." **Matthew 26:47-52, 54-56 NIV**

Jesus Before the Sanhedrin (Religious Leaders)

"Those who had arrested Jesus took him to Caiaphas, the high priest, where the teachers of the law and the elders had assembled. But Peter followed him at a distance, right

up to the courtyard of the high priest. He entered and sat down with the guards to see the outcome.

The chief priests and the whole Sanhedrin were looking for false evidence against Jesus so that they could put him to death. But they did not find any, though many false witnesses came forward. Finally, two came forward and declared, "This fellow said, 'I am able to destroy the temple of God and rebuild it in three days.'" Then the high priest stood up and asked Jesus, "Are you not going to answer?

What is this testimony that these men are bringing against you?" But Jesus remained silent. The high priest told him, "I charge you under oath by the living God: Tell us if you are the Messiah, the Son of God." "You have said so," Jesus replied. "But I say to all of you: From now on, you will see the Son of Man sitting at the right hand of the Mighty One and coming on the clouds of heaven."

Then the high priest tore his clothes and said, "He has spoken blasphemy! Why do we need any more witnesses? Look, now you have heard the blasphemy. What do you think?" "He is worthy of death," they answered. Then they spit in his face and struck him with their fists. Others slapped him."
"And said, "Prophesy to us, Messiah. Who hit you?""

Peter Disowns Jesus

"Now Peter was sitting out in the courtyard, and a servant girl came to him. "You also were with Jesus of Galilee," she said. But he denied it before them all. "I don't

know what you're talking about," he said. Then he went to the gateway, where another servant girl saw him and said to the people there, "This fellow was with Jesus of Nazareth." He denied it again with an oath: "I don't know the man!" After a little while, those standing there went up to Peter and said, "Surely you are one of them; your accent gives you away." Then he began to call down curses and swore to them, "I don't know the man!" Immediately, a rooster crowed. Then Peter remembered the word Jesus had spoken: "Before the rooster crows, you will disown me three times." And he went outside and wept bitterly."
Matthew 26:57-75 NIV

Judas Hangs Himself

"Early in the morning, all the chief priests and the elders of the people made their plans on how to have Jesus executed. So they bound him, led him away, and handed him over to Pilate, the governor. When Judas, who had betrayed him, saw that Jesus was condemned, he was seized with remorse and returned the thirty pieces of silver to the chief priests and the elders. "I have sinned," he said, "for I have betrayed innocent blood."

"What is that to us?" they replied, "That's your responsibility." So Judas threw the money into the temple and left. Then he went away and hanged himself. The chief priests picked up the coins and said, "It is against the law to put this into the treasury since it is blood money." So they decided to use the money to buy the potter's field as a burial place for foreigners.

Then what was spoken by Jeremiah, the prophet, was

*fulfilled: "They took the thirty pieces of silver, the price set on him by the people of Israel, and they used them to buy the potter's field, as the Lord commanded me." **Matthew 27:1-7, 9-10 NIV***

Jesus Before Pilot

"Then the Jewish leaders took Jesus from Caiaphas to the palace of the Roman governor. By now, it was early morning, and to avoid ceremonial uncleanness, they had not entered the palace because they wanted to be able to eat the Passover. So Pilate came out to them and asked, "What charges are you bringing against this man?" "If he were not a criminal," they replied, "we would not have handed him over to you."

Pilate said, "Take him yourselves and judge him by your own law." "But we have no right to execute anyone," they objected. This took place to fulfill what Jesus had said about the kind of death he was going to die. Pilate then went back inside the palace, summoned Jesus, and asked him, "Are you the king of the Jews?" "Is that your idea," Jesus asked, "or did others talk to you about me?" "Am I a Jew?" Pilate replied. "Your own people and chief priests handed you over to me.

What is it you have done?" Jesus said, "My kingdom is not of this world. If it were, my servants would fight to prevent my arrest by the Jewish leaders. But now my kingdom is from another place." "You are a king, then!" said Pilate. Jesus answered, "You say that I am a king. In fact, the reason I was born and came into the world is to testify to the truth. Everyone on the side of truth listens to me." "What is truth?" retorted Pilate.

With this, he went out again to the Jews gathered there and said, "I find no basis for a charge against him. But it is your custom for me to release to you one prisoner at the time of the Passover. Do you want me to release 'the king of the Jews'?" They shouted back, "No, not him! Give us Barabbas!" Now Barabbas had taken part in an uprising." John 18:28-40 NIV

"Meanwhile, Jesus stood before the governor, and the governor asked him, "Are you the king of the Jews?" "You have said so," Jesus replied. When he was accused by the chief priests and the elders, he did not answer. Then Pilate asked him, "Don't you hear the testimony they are bringing against you?" But Jesus made no reply, not even to a single charge—to the great amazement of the governor.

Now, the governor's custom at the festival was to release a prisoner chosen by the crowd. At that time, they had a well-known prisoner named Jesus Barabbas. So when the crowd had gathered, Pilate asked them, "Which one do you want me to release to you: Jesus Barabbas, or Jesus, who is called the Messiah?" For he knew it was out of self-interest that they had handed Jesus over to him. While Pilate was sitting in the judge's seat, his wife sent him this message: "Don't have anything to do with that innocent man, for I have suffered a great deal today in a dream because of him."

But the chief priests and the elders persuaded the crowd to ask for Barabbas and to have Jesus executed. "Which of the two do you want me to release to you?"

asked the governor. "Barabbas," they answered. "What shall I do with Jesus, who is called the Messiah?" Pilate asked. They all answered, "Crucify him!" "Why? What crime has he committed?" asked Pilate. But they shouted all the louder, "Crucify him!" When Pilate saw that he was getting nowhere but that instead, an uproar was starting, he took water and washed his hands in front of the crowd.

Judas wasn't the only one who betrayed Jesus; he was the closest one to Jesus to betray him. Many of the same people who shouted" Hosanna" when Jesus entered the city five days later were shouting "Crucify Him!" People will turn on you when they don't love you. They had no love for the Lord. Jesus was not what they thought he should be and did not give them what they imagined. They didn't want a Savior, they didn't want a prophet, they wanted a king now, not a king later…so, "Crucify Him!"

Some people follow you because of what they think you are and what they can get from you. If you disappoint them, they will turn on you and lie to you, seeking to destroy you simply because you did not finance their fantasy. Don't be surprised at people who turn on you because you did not give them the life they imagined you would.

Betrayal can hide in people for as long as it takes. Some good people have lost their lives, and some even have been imprisoned simply because someone they loved didn't love them in the way they gave them love and was disappointed. We may love Jesus, but for Judas and these people…Jesus was a disappointment.

"I am innocent of this man's blood," he said. "It is

*your responsibility!" All the people answered, "His blood is on us and our children!" Then he released Barabbas to them, but he had Jesus flogged and handed him over to be crucified." **Matthew 27:11-26 NIV***

Jesus Is Mocked

Be encouraged, kingdom family, when people mock you for what you believe. Stand on what God's word says; one day, they will not be mocking anymore. They will wish they had listened and walked the walk you're being mocked for; so many who have presided over us in death are in darkness and hopelessness right now. Trust and believe they are in that holding place right now at this very moment, thinking about all the things you said to them and how they treated you. This is why Jesus tells us to pray for our enemies. We should want anyone to go to that place...

*"Then the governor's soldiers took Jesus into the Praetorium and gathered the whole company of soldiers around him. They stripped him and put a scarlet robe on him and then twisted together a crown of thorns and set it on his head. They put a staff in his right hand. Then they knelt in front of him and mocked him. "Hail, king of the Jews!" they said. They spit on him, took the staff, and struck him on the head again and again. After they had mocked him, they took off the robe and put his own clothes on him. Then they led him away to crucify him."**Matthew 27:27-31 NIV***

Jesus Sentenced to Be Crucified

"Then Pilate took Jesus and had him flogged. The

soldiers twisted together a crown of thorns and put it on his head. They clothed him in a purple robe and went up to him again and again, saying, "Hail, king of the Jews!" And they slapped him in the face. Once more, Pilate came out and said to the Jews gathered there, "Look, I am bringing him out to you to let you know that I find no basis for a charge against him."

When Jesus came out wearing the crown of thorns and the purple robe, Pilate said to them, "Here is the man!" When the chief priests and their officials saw him, they shouted, "Crucify! Crucify!" But Pilate answered, "You take him and crucify him. As for me, I find no basis for a charge against him." The Jewish leaders insisted, "We have a law, and according to that law, he must die because he claimed to be the Son of God." When Pilate heard this, he was even more afraid, "Do you refuse to speak to me?" Pilate said. "Don't you realize I have power either to free you or to crucify you?"

Jesus answered, "You would have no power over me if it were not given to you from above. Therefore, the one who handed me over to you is guilty of a greater sin." From then on, Pilate tried to set Jesus free, but the Jewish leaders kept shouting, "If you let this man go, you are no friend of Caesar. Anyone who claims to be a king opposes Caesar." When Pilate heard this, he brought Jesus out and sat down on the judge's seat at a place known as the Stone Pavement (which in Aramaic is Gabbatha).

It was the day of Preparation for the Passover; it was about noon. "Here is your king," Pilate said to the Jews. But they shouted, "Take him away! Take him away! Crucify him!" "Shall I crucify your king?" Pilate asked. "We have no king but Caesar," the chief priests answered. Finally, Pilate handed him over to them to be crucified. So the soldiers took charge of Jesus." **John 19:1-8, 10-16 NIV**

The Crucifixion of Jesus

"Carrying his own cross, he went out to the place of the Skull (which in Aramaic is called Golgotha). There, they crucified him and with him two others—one on each side and Jesus in the middle. Pilate had a notice prepared and fastened to the cross. It read: Jesus of Nazareth, the king of the Jews. Many of the Jews read this sign, for the place where Jesus was crucified was near the city, and the sign was written in Aramaic, Latin, and Greek.

The chief priests of the Jews protested to Pilate, "Do not write, 'The King of the Jews,' but that this man claimed to be king of the Jews." Pilate answered, "What I have written, I have written." When the soldiers crucified Jesus, they took his clothes, dividing them into four shares, one for each of them, with the undergarment remaining. This garment was seamless, woven in one piece from top to bottom. "Let's not tear it," they said to one another. "Let's decide by lot who will get it."

This happened that the scripture might be fulfilled that said, "They divided my clothes among them and cast lots for my garment." So this is what the soldiers did. Near the cross of Jesus stood his mother, his mother's sister, Mary, the wife of Clopas, and Mary Magdalene. When Jesus saw his mother there and the disciple whom he loved standing nearby, he said to her, "Woman, here is your son," and to *the disciple, "Here is your mother." From that time on, this disciple took her into his home." **John 19:17-27 NIV***

"As they were going out, they met a man from Cyrene named Simon, and they forced him to carry the cross. They came to a place called Golgotha (which means "the place of the skull"). There, they offered Jesus wine mixed with gall to drink, but after tasting it, he refused to drink it.

When they had crucified him, they divided up his clothes by casting lots. And sitting down, they kept watch over him there. Above his head, they placed the written charge against him: this is Jesus, the king of the Jews. Two rebels were crucified with him, one on his right and one on his left. Those who passed by hurled insults at him, shaking their heads. In the same way, the chief priests, the teachers of the law, and the elders mocked him. "He saved others," they said, "But he can't save himself!

*He's the king of Israel! Let him come down now from the cross, and we will believe in him. He trusts in God. Let God rescue him now if he wants him, for he said, 'I am the Son of God.' " In the same way, the rebels who were crucified with him also heaped insults on him." **Matthew 27:32-39, 41-44 NIV***

The Death of Jesus

From noon until three afternoon, darkness came over all the land. About three in the afternoon, Jesus cried out in a loud voice, "Eli, Eli, lema sabachthani?" (which means "My God, my God, why have you forsaken me?"). When some of those standing there heard this, they said, "He's calling Elijah."

Immediately, one of them ran and got a sponge. He filled it with wine vinegar, put it on a staff, and offered it to Jesus to drink. The rest said, "Now leave him alone. Let's see if Elijah comes to save him." And when Jesus had cried out again in a loud voice, he gave up his spirit. At that moment, the temple curtain was torn from top to bottom. The earth shook, the rocks split, and the tombs broke open. The bodies of many holy people who had died were raised to life.

After Jesus' resurrection, they emerged from the tombs, entered the holy city, and appeared to many people. When the centurion and those with him guarding Jesus saw the earthquake and all that had happened, they were terrified and exclaimed, "Surely he was the Son of God!"

Many women were there, watching from a distance. They had followed Jesus from Galilee to care for his needs. Among them were Mary Magdalene, Mary the mother of James and Joseph, and the mother of Zebedee's sons." **Matthew 27:45-56 NIV**

"Later, knowing that everything had now been finished, and so that Scripture would be fulfilled, Jesus said, "I am thirsty." A jar of wine vinegar was there, so they soaked a sponge in it, put the sponge on a stalk of the hyssop plant, and lifted it to Jesus' lips. When he had received the drink, Jesus said, "It is finished."

With that, he bowed his head and gave up his spirit. Now, it was the day of Preparation, and the next day was to be a special Sabbath. Because the Jewish leaders did not want the bodies left on the crosses during the Sabbath, they asked Pilate to have the legs broken and the bodies taken down.

The soldiers, therefore, came and broke the legs of the first man who had been crucified with Jesus and then those of the other. But when they came to Jesus and found that he was already dead, they did not break his legs. Instead, one of the soldiers pierced Jesus' side with a spear, bringing a sudden flow of blood and water.

The man who saw it has given testimony, and his testimony is true. He knows that he tells the truth, testifies so that you also may believe, and, as another scripture says, "They will look on the one they have pierced." **John 19:28-35, 37 NIV**

"And blessed is he, whosoever shall not, be offended with me." Mathew 11:6

It was the Cross at Calvary that gave us access....Now access has been granted...hallelujah!

CHAPTER SIX
The Resurrection

When you hear the word **Resurrection,** what is your first thought?

When we think God is too late…

Lazarus was sick…very sick. His sisters Martha and Mary continually prayed for their brother for a miracle. This was the same Mary who wept at Jesus' feet and dried his feet with her hair. Jesus loved them, and they loved Him. At this time, she was hurt because Jesus did not get there when she thought he should have. She was disappointed in the fact that her brother died, and not only did Jesus not come to pray for him, but he didn't even make the funeral.

After he said this, he told them, "Our friend Lazarus has fallen asleep, but I am going there to wake him up." His disciples replied, "Lord, if he sleeps, he will get better." So then he told them plainly, "Lazarus is dead. Then Thomas (also known as Didymus) said to the rest of the disciples, "Let us also go, that we may die with him."

On his arrival, Jesus found that Lazarus had already been in the tomb for four days. And many Jews had come to Martha and Mary to comfort them in the loss of their brother. When Martha heard that Jesus was coming, she went to meet him, but Mary stayed home. "Lord," Martha said to Jesus, "if you had been here, my brother would not have died. Jesus said to her, "Your brother will rise again." Martha answered, "I know he will rise again in the **resurrection** *on the last day."*

Jesus said to her, **"I am the resurrection and the life.** *The one who believes in me will live, even though they die; "Yes, Lord," she replied, "I believe that you are the Messiah, the Son of God, who is to come into the world." After she said this, she returned and called her sister Mary aside. "The Teacher is here," she said, "and is asking for you." Now, Jesus had not yet entered the village but was still at the place where Martha had met him.*

When the Jews who had been with Mary in the house, comforting her, noticed how quickly she got up and went out, they followed her, supposing she was going to the tomb to mourn there. When Mary reached the place where Jesus was and saw him, she fell at his feet and said, "Lord, if you had been here, my brother would not have died." When Jesus saw her weeping, and the Jews who had come along with her also weeping, he was deeply moved in spirit and troubled.

"Where have you laid him?" he asked. "Come and see Lord," they replied. Jesus wept. Then the Jews said, "See how he loved him!" But some of them said, "Could not he who opened the eyes of the blind man have kept this man from dying?" John 11:11-12, 14, 16-17, 19-21, 23-25, 27-28, 30-37

We have been taught or conditioned to think the resurrection is an event, something we are waiting for, that can only happen on a scheduled date. She repeatedly said, "On that day," believing Jesus could heal him but thinking he's more than even that; he's the Resurrection and life! How powerful is it for him to be there? Even reading how Jesus wept shows he's in tune and touch with his people. I refuse to believe Jesus was crying because of Lazarus' death because he called it "Sleeping," but I believe he was touched by their mourning and pain, weeping as those who had no hope.

However, the greater part of Jesus weeping was because there were two great and influential groups of priesthood present, the Pharisees and Sadducees. There were divisions among the two groups of leaders. The Pharisees believed in the resurrection, but the Sadducees said, "There's no such thing as resurrection." Here they were at Lazarus's funeral. They were looking for Jesus to see how to arrest him; they were desperately trying to catch him doing wrong or breaking the Law of Moses. They said, "He loves Lazarus; could he come to heal him because he loves him?

"Jesus, once more deeply moved, came to the tomb. It was a cave with a stone laid across the entrance. "Take away the stone," he said. "But, Lord," said Martha, the sister of the dead man, "by this time, there is a bad odor, for he has been there four days." Then Jesus said, "Did I not tell you that if you believe, you will see the glory of God?" So they took away the stone.

Then Jesus looked up and said, "Father, I thank

you that you have heard me. When he said this, Jesus loudly said, "Lazarus, come out!" The dead man came out, his hands and feet wrapped with strips of linen and a cloth around his face. Jesus told them, "Take off the grave clothes and let him go." John 11:38-41, 43-44

"Therefore, many of the Jews who had come to visit Mary and had seen what Jesus did believed in him. However, some of them went to the Pharisees and were told what Jesus had done. Then, the chief priests and the Pharisees called a meeting of the Sanhedrin. "What are we accomplishing?" they asked. "Here is this man performing many signs. If we let him go on like this, everyone will believe in him, and then the Romans will come and take away both our temple and our nation."

Then one of them, named Caiaphas, who was high priest that year, spoke up, "You know nothing at all! You do not realize that it is better for you that one man die for the people than that the whole nation perish." He did not say this on his own, but as a high priest that year, he prophesied that Jesus would die for the Jewish nation, and not only for that nation but also for the scattered children of God, to bring them together and make them one.

Therefore, Jesus no longer publicly moved about among the people of Judea. Instead, he withdrew to a region near the wilderness, to a village called Ephraim, where he stayed with his disciples. When it was almost time for the Jewish Passover, many went up from the country to Jerusalem for their ceremonial cleansing before the Passover.

They kept looking for Jesus, and as they stood in the

temple courts, they asked one another, "What do you think? Isn't he coming to the festival at all?" But the chief priests and the Pharisees had given orders that anyone who found out where Jesus was should report it so they might arrest him."
  (John 11:45-52, 54-57)

"For as in Adam all die, so in Christ all will be made alive." 1 Corinthians 15:22 NIV.

"He is not here; he has risen, just as he said. Come and see the place where he lay." Matthew 28:6 NIV.

"But Christ has indeed been raised from the dead, the first fruits of those who have fallen asleep."
  1 Corinthians 15:20 NIV

For since death came through a man, the resurrection of the dead comes also through a man."
  1 Corinthians 15:21 NIV

"Jesus told her, "I am the resurrection and the life. The one who believes in me will live, even though they die;"
  John 11:25 NIV

"For we believe that Jesus died and rose again, and so we believe that God will bring with Jesus those who have fallen asleep in him."
  1 Thessalonians 4:14 NIV

"For my Father's will is that everyone who looks to the Son and believes in him shall have eternal life, and I will raise them up at the last day."

John 6:40 NIV

"By his power, God raised the Lord from the dead, and he will raise us also." 1 Corinthians 6:14 NIV

"Praise be to the God and Father of our Lord Jesus Christ! In his great mercy, he has given us new birth into a living hope through the resurrection of Jesus Christ from the dead," and into an inheritance that can never perish, spoil, or fade.

This inheritance is kept in heaven for you, who, through faith, are shielded by God's power until the coming of salvation, which is ready to be revealed in the last time. In all this, you greatly rejoice, though now, for a little while, you may have suffered grief in all kinds of trials. These have come so that the proven genuineness of your faith—of greater worth than gold, which perishes even though refined by fire—may result in praise, glory, and honor when Jesus Christ is revealed.

Though you have not seen him, you love him, and even though you do not see him now, you believe in him and are filled with inexpressible and glorious joy, for you are receiving the end result of your faith, the salvation of your souls." 1 Peter 1:4-9 NIV

If we have been united with him in a death like his, we will certainly be united with him in a resurrection like his." Romans 6:5 NIV

The Burial of Jesus

"Later, Joseph of Arimathea asked Pilate for the body of Jesus. Joseph was a secret disciple of Jesus because he feared the Jewish leaders. With Pilate's permission, he came and took the body away. He was accompanied by Nicodemus, the man who had visited Jesus earlier that night.

Nicodemus brought a mixture of myrrh and aloes, about seventy-five pounds. Taking Jesus' body, the two of them wrapped it with the spices in linen strips. This was in accordance with Jewish burial customs. At the place where Jesus was crucified, there was a garden, and in the garden, there was a new tomb in which no one had ever been laid. Because it was the Jewish day of Preparation and since the tomb was nearby, they laid Jesus there."John 19:38-42 NIV

He placed it in his new tomb, which he had cut out of the rock. He rolled a big stone in front of the entrance to the tomb and went away. Mary Magdalene and the other Mary were sitting there opposite the tomb."Matthew 27:60-61 NIV

Guarding the Tomb

"The next day, the one after Preparation Day, the chief priests and the Pharisees went to Pilate. "Sir," they said, "we remember that while he was still alive, that deceiver said, 'After three days, I will rise again.' So, give the order for the tomb to be made secure until the third day.

Otherwise, his disciples may come and steal the body and tell the people that he has been raised from the dead. This last deception will be worse than the first." "Take a guard," Pilate answered. "Go, make the tomb as secure as you know how." Matthew 27:62-65 NIV

The Empty Tomb

Early on the first day of the week, while it was still dark, Mary Magdalene went to the tomb and saw that the stone had been removed from the entrance. So she ran to Simon Peter and the other disciple, the one Jesus loved, and said, "They have taken the Lord out of the tomb, and we don't know where they have put him!" So Peter and the other disciples started for the tomb.

So Peter and the other disciples started for the tomb. Both were running, but the other disciple outran Peter and reached the tomb first. He bent over and looked in at the strips of linen lying there but did not go in. Then Simon Peter came along behind him and went straight into the tomb. He saw the strips of linen lying there and the cloth wrapped around Jesus' head. The cloth was still lying in its place, separate from the linen.

Finally, the other disciple, who had reached the tomb first, went inside. He saw and believed. (They still did not understand from Scripture that Jesus had to rise from the dead.) Then, the disciples went back to where they were staying. Now Mary stood outside the tomb crying. As she wept, she bent over to look into the tomb and saw two white angels seated where Jesus' body had been, one at the head and the other at the foot.

They asked her, "Woman, why are you crying?" "They have taken my Lord away," she said, "and I don't know where they have put him." At this, she turned around and saw Jesus standing there but did not realize it was Jesus. He asked her, "Woman, why are you crying? Who is it you are looking for?" Thinking he was the gardener, she said, "Sir, if you have carried him away, tell me where you have put him, and I will get him." Jesus said to her, "Mary." She turned toward him and cried out in Aramaic, "Rabboni!" (which means "Teacher").

Jesus said, "Do not hold on to me, for I have not yet ascended to the Father. Go instead to my brothers and tell them, 'I am ascending to my Father and your Father, to my God and your God.' " Mary Magdalene went to the disciples with the news: "I have seen the Lord!" And she told them that he had said these things to her." John 20:1-18 NIV

Jesus Has Risen

"After the Sabbath, at dawn on the first day of the week, Mary Magdalene and the other Mary went to look at the tomb. There was a violent earthquake, for an angel of the Lord came down from heaven and, going to the tomb, rolled back the stone and sat on it. His appearance was like lightning, and his clothes were white as snow. The guards were so afraid of him that they shook and became like dead men. The angel said to the women, "Do not be afraid, for I know you are looking for Jesus, who was crucified. He is not here; he has risen, just as he said. Come and see the place where he lay." Matthew 28:1-6 NIV

The Resurrection

"The first day of the week cometh Mary Magdalene early, when it was yet dark, unto the Sepulchre, and sees the stone taken away from the Sepulchre. Then she runneth and cometh to Simon Peter, and to the other disciple, whom Jesus loved, and saith unto them,

They have taken away the Lord out of the Sepulchre, and we know not where they have laid him. Peter therefore went forth, and that other disciple, and came to the Sepulchre. So they ran together, and the other disciple outrun Peter and came first to the Sepulchre. He stooped down and looked in and saw the linen clothes lying, yet he did not go in.

Then cometh Simon Peter following him, and went into the Sepulchre, and sees the linen clothes lie, and the napkin, that was about his head, not lying with the linen clothes, but wrapped together in a place by itself. Then, that other disciple also went in, which came first to the Sepulchre, and he saw and believed. Yet they did not know that he must rise again from the dead. Then the disciples went away again unto their own home.

But Mary stood without at the Sepulchre weeping: and as she wept, she stooped down and looked into the Sepulchre, and saw two angels in white sitting, the one at the head, and the other at the feet, where the body of Jesus had lain. And they say unto her, Woman, why weepest thou? She saith unto them, Because they have taken away my Lord, and I know not where they have laid him. And when she had thus said, she turned herself back and saw Jesus standing, and knew not that it was Jesus.

* * *

Jesus saith unto her, Woman, why weepest thou? Whom seekest thou? She, supposing him to be the gardener, saith unto him, Sir, if thou have borne him hence, tell me where thou hast laid him, and I will take him away. Jesus saith unto her, Mary, she turned herself, and saith unto him, Rabboni; which is to say, Master. **Jesus saith unto her, Touch me not; for I am not yet ascended to my Father: but go to my brethren, and say unto them, I ascend unto my Father, and your Father; and to my God, and your God.**

Mary Magdalene came and told the disciples that she had seen the Lord and that he had spoken these things unto her. Then the same day in the evening, being the first day of the week, when the doors were shut where the disciples were assembled for fear of the Jews, came to Jesus and stood in the midst, and saith unto them, Peace be unto you. And when he had said, he showed them his hands and his side.

Then were the disciples glad when they saw the Lord. Then said Jesus to them again, Peace be unto you: as my Father hath sent me, even so send I you. And when he had said this, he breathed on them, and saith unto them, Receive ye the Holy Ghost: whose soever sins ye remit, they are remitted unto them; and whose soever sins ye retain, they are retained. But Thomas, one of the twelve, called Didymus, was not with them when Jesus came. The other disciples, therefore, said unto him, We have seen the Lord. But he said unto them, Except I shall see in his hands the print of the nails, put my finger into the print of the nails, and thrust my hand into his side; I will not believe.

After eight days again, his disciples were within, and

Thomas was with them. Then came Jesus, the doors being shut, and stood in the midst and said, Peace be unto you. Then saith he to Thomas, Reach thy finger hither, and behold my hands; and reach thy hand hither, and thrust it into my side; and be not faithless, but believing. And Thomas answered and said unto him, My Lord and my God. Jesus saith unto him, Thomas, because thou hast seen me, thou hast believed: blessed are they that have not seen, and yet have believed. And many other signs truly did Jesus in the presence of his disciples, which are not written in this book: but these are written, that ye might believe that Jesus is the Christ, the Son of God; and that believing ye might have life through his name."John 20:1-31 KJV

Jesus was the first to turn the grave (tomb) into a dressing room. When Jesus died, he said, "Father, into your hands I commit my spirit," and he passed away. His spirit went to the Father, his soul went into Hades (Hell/Paradise), and his body was laid in the tomb.

Look at our God; he is resurrected but takes the time to remove the stone that was used to close the mouth of the tomb. He didn't move to get it but moved it so that the women who came looking for him could get in. Then, before he exits, he takes the time to leave us, the church, a message by his grave clothes left behind. He also takes the time to fold the napkin wrapped around his head but leaves the linen wreaked around his body, unmade and unraveled, like an unmade bed. He was letting the disciples (man and female) know that You must get the church in order because me and my Father are ONE, unified (the head), but the body (church) has to come into the unity of the Holy Spirit., to be one.

* * *

Jesus knew that Satan would attack the Body of Christ with DIVISION, mainly…Denominations! There are stupid reasons for the "Body of Christ" to be divided over the baptism of water and spirit, of John or Jesus, of Paul or Peter, Baptist or Pentecostal, having the Holy Ghost or Not, necessary or not, women can preach, or ought not to preach, fasting or not fasting, speaking in tongues or no speaking in tongues, jew or gentile church, should women be silent or should they speak…you get the idea? We are divided on so many foolish things. Without Christ, there would be no "Body of Christ (The Church).

Look at what Jesus prayed well in advance before he was crucified, "My prayer is not for them alone. I pray also for those who will believe in me through their message, that all of them may be one, Father, just as you are in me and I am in you. May they also be in us so the world may believe you have sent me. I have given them the glory you gave me, that they may be one as we are one— I in them and you in me—so they may be brought to complete unity. Then the world will know that you sent me and have loved them even as you have loved me." John 17:20-23 NIV

We are three-part beings: spirit, soul, and body, created in the image of the triune God- the Father, Son, and Holy Spirit.

Jesus is Alive!

"They were talking with each other about everything that had happened. As they talked and discussed these things with each other, Jesus himself came up and walked

along with them, but they were kept from recognizing him. He asked them, "What are you discussing together as you walk along?" They stood still, their faces downcast. One of them, Cleopas, asked him, "Are you the only one visiting Jerusalem who does not know the things that have happened there these days?" "What things?" He asked. "About Jesus of Nazareth," they replied. "He was a prophet, powerful in word and deed before God and all the people. The chief priests and our rulers handed him over to be sentenced to death, and they crucified him, but we had hoped that he was the one who was going to redeem Israel.

And what is more, it is the third day since all this took place. In addition, some of our women amazed us. They went to the tomb early this morning but didn't find his body. They came and told us that they had seen a vision of angels who said he was alive. Then some of our companions went to the tomb and found it just as the women had said, but they did not see Jesus." He told them, "How foolish you are, and how slow to believe all the prophets have spoken! Did not the Messiah have to suffer these things and then enter his glory?"

And beginning with Moses and all the Prophets, he explained to them what was said in all the Scriptures concerning himself. As they approached the village they were going to, Jesus continued as if he were going farther. But they urged him strongly, "Stay with us, for it is nearly evening; the day is almost over." So he went in to stay with them. When he was at the table with them, he took bread, thanked them, broke it, and began to give it to them. Then their eyes were opened, and they recognized him, but he disappeared.

They asked each other, "Were not our hearts burning within us while he talked with us on the road and opened the Scriptures to us?" They got up and returned at once to Jerusalem. There, they found the Eleven and those with them, assembled together and saying, "It is true! The Lord has risen and has appeared to Simon." Then the two told what had happened on the way and how they recognized Jesus when he broke the bread."Luke 24:14-35 NIV

After everything Jesus went through for you and me, we can never take him for granted…at least, we ought not to. When we see how Jesus was abused, betrayed, mocked, hated, and killed, don't ever think because of your struggles, and being hated causes you to think less of yourself. Pick your head up in humility and honor. Know this: you will never die believing in The Lord Jesus Christ.

Do not be afraid. Home is beautiful, and you have true family there cheering you on. We were never meant to be here without this fight. God can't trust us until we have tried in time. Eternity is where you want to be; you may not know it yet. True the Lord with all of your heart. Be relentless, steadfast, and unmovable.

We live in intruding times but know they will not last forever. Your real life is a continuation of your dreams and ambitions. Do business and God's business while you're here, but by no means get caught up in this world; Satan will swallow you up and laugh at you in the process! He's been doing this for a long time. Don't be one to share in his JUDGMENT! Choose today who you are going to serve. God or Money, Good or evil, right or wrong, weak or wicked, life or death?

I know people who have chosen this world and material things over God. They practice religion while selling out for this world. Amazingly, they are nowhere near rich but have sold their souls like Judas for a quick high or good feeling they cannot keep. I call it **"Dying for Memories."** What could we say on Judgment Day? That we didn't know, or we didn't think it was this serious? ...And He says, "Call on the god that you served in your lifetime."

When Jesus defeated Death, hell, and the grave, he collected the keys that would free you and me. Have you noticed that God never proves Himself to the wicked, only to His children, those who believe in Him? No one can come remotely close to what God has done for us. So, I choose JESUS!

"But if the Spirit of him that raised up Jesus from the dead dwell in you, he that raised up Christ from the dead shall also quicken your mortal bodies by his Spirit that dwells in you."
Romans 8:11 KJV

There is so much proof of who Jesus was to their generation and every generation from the past, present, and future. Death is not the End for a believer; rather, it's a continuation of life, your best life yet, that you've never accurately imagined. *But as it is written, Eye hath not seen, nor ear heard, Neither have entered into the heart of man, The things which God hath prepared for them that love him." 1 Corinthians 2:9 KJV.*

* * *

When people make a mockery of you as a believer and say, "Isn't Jesus supposed to be coming back? When is he coming? You Christians have been saying this forever, and He still hasn't come back…I'm waiting to see him too… keep waiting for him…hahaha.

They have no clue. Every time a person or persons take their last breath, oh, they get to see him! This is the whole purpose of the book. Take away the foolishness of death is over; no, death is just the beginning of dealing with the One who created you! Whether you believe it or not, it carries no wait. You don't have to believe in death, but keep on living until you expire, and then what? Jesus had to say this to a few who thought they knew more than God.

Check this out!
"And he said unto me, Seal not the sayings of the prophecy of this book; for the time is at hand. He who is unjust, let him be unjust still; and he who is filthy, let him be filthy still; and he who is righteous, let him be righteous still; and he who is holy, let him be holy still. And, behold, I come quickly; and my reward is with me, to give every man according as his work shall be.

I am Alpha and Omega, the beginning, the end, the first, and the last. Blessed are they that do his commandments, that they may have right to the tree of life and enter through the gates into the city. For without are dogs, and sorcerers, and whoremongers, and murderers, and idolaters, and whosoever loves and makes a lie."
Revelation 22:10-15 KJV
As soon as you take your last breath…

If I never have the pleasure of meeting you here in this life and world, let's be united with love and faith in our Lord Jesus Christ and continue to preach the gospel of the kingdom. Love one another, strive to make this world a better place for our children, and save as many people as possible; I know it gets hard sometimes!

"We can do all things..through Christ who strengthens us"…Right!

These things were left on record, which we might believe.

Know your Kingdom Rights!

I'll see you on the other side of this…SELAH

Jesus Is The Resurrection!

CHAPTER SEVEN
Easter Morning

It's Wednesday before Easter Sunday, and I'm waiting on a package…it's late. Finally, I received it, and it's all there and good. I have my people, and they are very anxious to get their hands on this product. I wanted to believe that I was just worried about the money it would bring me, but this was not true. I was hooked! I was a drug (cocaine) addict in denial. I had a secret! I had tried many times on my own to stop doing the dope thing but was unsuccessful.

Unknowingly, this would become the downward spiral, the scariest and worst time of my life! I was always a happy, upbeat person. I love life and music, and music has been my companion since age 11. It was Wednesday, and I felt good about the rest of the week. I was going to work as scheduled, but something appeared to be off. To get the jest of what happened, let me take you a little ways back to November before Easter.

I was weighing, cutting, packaging, and preparing for sales with my crew. We are about to hit the streets with one of the best products. While I'm standing at the table looking at all this patiently money to be made. Out of nowhere, I feel a presence like a warm blanket, like liquid coming down over me from the top of my head. As this is happening to me, it is as though someone controls the sound around me. The noise, music, and voices are becoming muffled and almost silent. Then I heard a voice speak to me in a calm I'd never experienced or heard of before.

The voice said, " I have anointed you and called you." Then I replied, " Well, why am I here in this place, doing these things?" Then He replied, " I AM going to deliver you and take you out of this; you will be a witness." Immediately, I began to cry, and I had no control. First, I looked around to see if anyone was seeing what was happening to me, or better yet, if they could hear me and this voice. Does anybody know? I'm starting to feel embarrassed because here I am, portraying the life of a drug dealer, and I'm over here crying like a baby. What?

Amazingly, no one noticed or attempted to talk to me during this encounter. This was another odd occurrence because someone was always saying or wanting something from me. I gave out packages to hit the streets. By Thursday night, I started getting high by smoking and sniffing cocaine. I was drinking hard liquor with a vengeance. I was wondering what was wrong with me. I couldn't stop! This drug thing is like a Secret Society. So many people do drugs; it's unbelievable. I think that's what drew me in. I thought drugs were for low-lives, and then I saw professional people doing it. Upper-class people...wow! I had a secret. I was doing drugs, and not many people knew about it except those who did it as well.

It's November, and we have about two weeks before Thanksgiving. Holidays were always big with my family, but I was feeling a little awkward because drugs were becoming my most significant concern. I love family, but this dope is calling me, and I'm shocked it has so much power over my life. It's as though I'm walking around with a personal drug-dealing, drug-using advisor in my head.

This goes around, and everybody is struggling with moving products. I was having some strange things happening. I couldn't help but think about what happened to me in the basement at the table. Could this be God messing with me? I can't explain it, but I started feeling some way about this. Re-up time was approaching, and I didn't see as much profit as the other times. I realized that, in time, I had become the biggest customer of my product. No matter how much you hear, Never get high on your supply," for whatever reason, you never think it will be you.

I began to lie to myself more frequently. "This time, I won't use much; I will get this money!" We're approaching Thanksgiving week, and now my excuse is we must enjoy the Holidays. After Thanksgiving Holidays, I realized how much money I was losing. I bought my first package with my construction company's money. In the beginning, it seemed brilliant. I was making money. From the beginning, I would always separate the money. I could see how much profit I was getting from the drugs.

I set a goal for myself that when December comes in, I will not get high again. I told myself, "You can do it," and it worsened. Secretly, I was getting scared. I thought of myself as a sober-minded, talented, and gifted person. I considered myself to be a pretty decent guy. I'm starting to feel like I'm losing control of my life. Now, I'm getting concerned; I haven't been able to stop this drug habit. I was always sober-minded, never smoked or drank, and didn't do drugs, but here I am. I'm starting to panic because I didn't know until now how addicted I was. I started thinking of the possibility of needing professional help. This made me think about my options, and I concluded I would stop this foolishness.

We're approaching the Christmas season, and I love Christmas. I love everything about it. The lights, the music, and the spirit of Christmas make me happy. It's the best time of the year. I took care of Christmas shopping early and now felt I could reward or treat myself—big mistake. I started getting high and just kept going.

My family, colleagues, and many friends had no clue that I was a working addict. I didn't miss work; I was on time, met my appointments, and appeared successful at my profession. I had my own business and thought I was more intelligent than most because I planned to invest in the dope game and flip my money into a profit. Well, that was the plan. It started with me making three times what I had initially invested.

I thought I was doing something new, not knowing how the enemy had mastered deception. For a moment, I was the man; at least, that's what they were saying. I felt like I was on top of the world, not knowing my world was about to come crashing down. I had a supernatural encounter in November of the previous year.

At this point, I have been doing cocaine and drinking alcohol for three days and night straight with no sleep. I had no appetite for food. I am so, so tired. I'm home now. I have a friend visiting from France, and she doesn't know that I do drugs. I met her when I was an active musician, and she's only known me as the clean-cut kind of guy. So, I'm reluctant to expose my drug indulging.

She's never even known me to drink alcohol. I can do away with the drinking; that wasn't my main thing; it was the sniffing and smoking of that cocaine that made me want to drink. We are hanging out, and I struggle to be who I am. The me I used to be. This messed with my ego and pride because I know how I was raised. I grew up in a drug-free home.

I grew up in church…I'm talking about the Pentecostal church! Where there was no drinking, no smoking, no cussing, and swearing, women didn't wear pants, and they were forbidden to wear jewelry except an engagement and wedding ring. …we were allowed to wear a watch but no bracelets or necklaces…Oh, I almost forgot. There are no earrings. My point is that I was the clean-due "Church Boy," as they would call me, as if that was my real name. I didn't drink or do drugs in school or when I was in bands traveling. I lived the club life for years and wouldn't touch a thing. I always ordered orange juice or gingerly from the bar…all the time. Bartenders knew me for that!

So here I am with this beautiful person who knows me from music, not church. She was clean-cut…" clean as a whistle," as they would say. This was one of the things that drew us together, as a staple of our newly found relationship at that time. I had a lot of respect for her, and now, I'm struggling to be who I used to be to her.

Well, it worked for a little while. When we were out to eat (well, I wasn't eating), I was thinking about my other date—cocaine! For a brief time, I liked how she reminded me of the guy who had gotten lost. I don't know if she knew, but I can't take it anymore. So, I excused myself from the table to go to the restroom. It's there where I had to get my (girl), as they used to call it. I went into the stall, and I'm telling you…I was sniffing that cocaine like there was no tomorrow! I returned to the table, and of course, I didn't want to touch my food. I was full of energy…to the max because I was always energized naturally, but no wit's turn up! I rushed her to get out of there and go home with me. This is where it became difficult to hide my addiction.

This was the beginning of my three-day binge. I was with her, but not with her, because I constantly excused myself to go to my bathroom. Finally, she asked me, "What are you doing? Is this not like you?" I paused for a second..and then said, "Look, I do a little cocaine; it's no big deal. She responded, "Wait a minute, Joseph, you get high now?" I was offended. Can you believe that….Was I offended? Once I overcame what I thought she might have felt about me getting, he "was on and popping," as they say. This would be the beginning of three days and nights getting high binge. I was getting high and drinking and sexing. How high can one get? It seems she accepted it; she did not condemn me; she acted as if this was ok…normal. She didn't mention my getting high again. What was sad and so wrong was by day number two, I pushed the cocaine on her."Don't let me do this by myself..come on…do it with me. I put it on my body and asked her to sniff it.

To all those who do drugs and have done drugs, you know it's the same story. The devil has no new tricks; he tries them on new people. I was so high my heart was hurting. I was high, and she was high. She didn't try smoking it, so I was the only one smoking. I was hitting that pipe over and over again. I wanted to rest. I wanted to stop! But I couldn't! There was a voice inside of me that was bigger than me. It keeps saying, "One more hit..you can do it."

At this point, I'm crying and hitting that glass pipe. All I can see is a smoke-filled bowl, and I'm thinking, how am I going to smoke all of that? I had plenty of it already rocked up and ready to go. I had powder and rock. I was starting to feel sick. The room was spinning, and my chest felt like a drum. I could hear it and feel it. I was scared, and this voice constantly told me to do more. I can't do more. I tell my friend that I need to sleep. I'm forcing myself to put down the pipe. I started walking around in the bedroom, but to no avail; I felt very anxious and strange. I think I might be having a Heart Attack, and I don't even know what that is. I attempted to calm myself down and get my friend scared. It feels like most of this is going on the inside of me. Why am I hearing these voices telling me it's okay? Should I do some more? "But I don't want to do more!" Who Am I talking to? All of this battle is going on inside of me. My friend does not have a clue.

"I just need some sleep," I said to my friend. "Okay, " she said. I lay down on the bed and closed my eyes. It felt like everything was moving and moving fast. I just wanted it to stop! As I lay there, my friend touched me, and I asked her to stop. "I need to sleep," I said. She said, "Okay." I was determined not to pick up that pipe. It appears these voices are taking turns convincing me to do more like it was their job or something. This was the worst day of my life. I was miserable! What started pro years of fun and a good time was now my misery. I began to ask God for help within myself; for some odd reason, I was afraid to say it aloud. I was pretty ashamed and condemned; I had not attended church in over ten years.

As I lay there, I felt like I was calming down. I couldn't help but think, can God hear my thoughts? I wonder? I kept my eyes closed as though it helped me not to see the drugs and the pipe. Maybe everything will be alright after all? I was starting to feel some peace…just a little bit. I had been getting high all night again, and dawn was about to break. I'm feeling crazy, but somehow I need it to be daytime. As I was lying there, I heard a different voice speaking in my ear; it was soft but with authority."Get Up! Today is the day of salvation," it said. First, I opened my eyes to see who was there because I heard this voice and could feel the breath of the mouth it came from. I jumped up and ran to my bathroom, turned on the water at the sink, and repeatedly threw cold water on my face.

Then, without drying my face, I looked into the mirror. It appeared that I was looking past myself; looking into my new eyes, I didn't see myself. I stared deeply, desperately trying to solve my mystery. For a minute, I forgot about the room, sleep, the drugs, my friend, and everything, even those demon voices that were trying to kill me. I looked at myself in the mirror and didn't like what I saw. I began to get closer to the mirror, trying to see who it was inside me because, I'm telling you, it was not me. Tears began to roll down my face as if it were on its own accord. I said to myself, "I can't do this anymore."

* * *

I dried my face and didn't have the answer, but I needed a change in my life. I began to lay down on the bed, and my friend asked, " Are you ok?" "Yes, I'm good," I said, although I wasn't. Now I'm thinking, What did I see in my eyes when I looked into the mirror? My eyes are closed again, but I feel differently about myself this time. I'm still wondering what were those choices of words said to me. "Day of salvation" what could it mean? I'm feeling enough peace and calm where I feel like I can go to sleep. I felt like I was beginning to get some sleep when I felt a vigorous tap on my shoulder and heard a voice at the same time say, "Get up, go to church; today is the day of salvation!"

I jumped up this time; looking around, my heart was racing. I'm thinking, ghosts, demons, or something? My friend asked, "What's the matter?... What's wrong?"Did you hear that? Did you feel that?"I asked."I didn't hear or feel anything; what are you talking about?" she said. I was thinking, I'm tripping from these drugs; now I'm hearing voices, seeing things, and feeling things. I need help. I ran to the bathroom, and this time, I was taking a look at myself. I wanted to see what I saw earlier. I began to stare at myself in the mirror. I have never experienced anything like this before. What is going on? I'm genuinely disturbed right now. I can still feel the fingers on my shoulders where whatever touched me. I stayed in the bathroom, trying to make heads or tails of what was happening to me.

I went to talk to my friend and asked her if she didn't mind leaving. I felt terrible, but I was going through something. She asked, "What's wrong, what's happening?" I said, " I need to go to church." "Go to church, She said," after all that we've been doing?""I know, right? I can't explain right now; I need to go," I said. She got up and got herself together. I gave her the bathroom, and we made plans to meet later that evening. She had a friend here in the States from Switzerland, and I assured her we would hook up and have a party. "So we'll talk later today," she said. "Sure thing,' I said.

I went back upstairs to jump in the shower and get dressed. I had so much running through my mind at the time. For some reason, I was feeling nervous. I had not attended church in years; I didn't know how to dress. My mind went back to when I was a teen. I know I'm expected to wear a suit and tie. I'm in my room looking for a suit to wear and turn on the TV. While looking in the closet, I heard this song. It made me stop everything and sit at the foot of the bed. I listened to this angelic voice singing. This man was singing my life through song. I could hardly believe it! It was so orchestrated that I could hear sounds all around me. I was looking around as if they were in my room right there with me, and I listened to these words;

Straighten My Life Out (The Winans), written and led vocals by Marvin Winans.

The way they repeatedly said, "Straighten my life out," was tearing me apart! It's been many years, and I can still feel the Holy Spirit in my hands while typing this. Those brothers and **Bishop Marvin Winans** were instrumental in saving my life. God used them and Marvin directly through song. It was as though he laid hands on me. Around all of those drugs in my house, and I had no desire to touch any of it after being ministered to in song. The lyrics preached to me, but Marvin's song delivery convicted me, not condemned me. ***Thank you, Brother Marvin, Carvin, Michael, and I salute my brother Ronald and Dad...Pop Winans*** are in Heaven having a good time; there are no words to express how much joy they are having all the time. He's "One of the One's Who Did." If I never get to see you here, I will get to see you home and tell you, " You may never know how many people you have reached?"

Imagine hearing something like this right after you hear, "Get up and go to church!" The lyrics were right on point and unbelievable. I was crying like a baby; I was in total disbelief. I was crying after the song went off TV and was looking around, like, are you for real? Less than two hours ago, I was holding my chest, thinking I was having a heart attack, and now this brother just took me to church in my bedroom. It felt like my bedroom had become a sanctuary for God. I didn't want to hear anything else on TV. I turned it off, still sobbing, because this man sang that song from the depths of his heart and soul. He made me feel like I could go to God for anything. They (the Winans) helped me to have the courage to walk through that church door. Now I was dressed and ready.

I went to my car and had a dilemma; I didn't know what church to attend. My first thought is the church I used to participate in from 11 years old, but I don't know what I would say. I was HIGH! Three days with no sleep, except maybe the ten minutes I was trying to get earlier before God disturbed me. Sometimes, I would wonder if I would have a cardiac arrest trying to sleep. Only God knows! I truly believe that God warns us and gives us a chance to reconcile with Him, but we must choose. I chose to see the signs, hear the signs, and believe the signs, and I got up as instructed.

As I am driving, I hear within me a calm spirit of a voice telling me to go to my Family's church. I thought, "I don't want them to see me in this condition. I cleaned up pretty well, but three days, no sleep, constantly getting high. But, again, I am obeying the good voice telling me to go to my family's church. When I arrived in the parking lot, I was shaking; I was so nervous. I'm thinking, what will they say or think? Will they see in me that I saw in the bathroom at my house? I feel different after hearing that song, "Straighten My Life Out."

I parked the car, and here goes. I'm walking up the steps and approaching the front door. I can see some people, but mainly two people ready to open the door to greet me. To my surprise, one of the gentlemen to speak to me was an usher. He was dressed in a suit, wore white gloves, and was very polite to me. He said, " What are you doing here this morning?" I was shocked! I asked him what he was doing in the church and not just that, but working as an usher. He said, "I've been here for over three years now, and I have been cleaned from drugs." Then he said, "Man, I can't believe you are in church, and I am going to take you to the front to be seated." Then I responded, "Whatever." He replied by asking, "Where would you like to be seated?" My response was, "It does not matter."

As we began to walk down the aisle to where I was to be seated, the pastor was already preaching, and I heard the Bible close (slam shut via the mic), and the pastor said, "God, just changed my message; **TODAY is the day of salvation for someone that is here.**" Then, to my surprise, this was the third time I had heard that phrase in one morning. Sitting in my seat, I couldn't help but feel God was giving me signs. The pastor began to preach about Jesus Christ, his love for people, why he came and died, and that God loves you no matter where you come from. The message was mainly about the Love of God and that you could go to him without problems.

I could not believe I was in church on Easter Sunday. When the pastor started to speak about how empty the tomb Jesus had been buried in was, he said he had risen and come to life. And because Jesus lives, we can live. Just as he grew, we can rise above any circumstances. The pastor proceeded to come down from the pulpit toward the main floor as she continued to speak. She was walking the aisles while preaching, and it was my life that she was talking about, and that caught my attention. She was not looking at me, but still, as she spoke, she was talking about my life and there were things that only God could know.

I couldn't help but feel that my whole morning was orchestrated and planned out somehow. I began to feel nervous for some reason and did not understand why at the time. The more she spoke, the more my life was revealed to me. Afterward, she made an altar call and asked if anyone needed to give their life to the Lord. Then I became nervous because I wanted to go and get prayer, but I felt ashamed because I was high for three days. People started to walk toward the altar for worship, and suddenly, I became severely nervous. I began to hear voices, the same voices that were talking to me, telling me to continue to smoke the cocaine.

* * *

They were trying to talk me out of going up to the altar and getting prayer, and for some reason, I could not move; I felt paralyzed. As the pastor prayed for other people, she continued speaking and asking if someone else needed prayer. And as I was looking, the altar was complete, and people were in line. A brother from the church tapped me and asked me, "Brother, would you like to come up with me to get prayer?" And I replied, "No, I am good." Even though I wanted to go, he replied, " Are you sure?" and I responded, "Yes." I put my head down as if I could side my shame because that is how I felt. I began to think that all eyes were on me, but that was not necessarily true.

I thought maybe I was paranoid, so I kept my head down for a minute, and between the prayers, the pastor kept saying, "Someone else needs to come up here for prayer." That caused me to look up to see if the prayer line was shorter, and I saw the brother in line asking me to go up with him to get prayer. Then the pastor said again, "Someone else needs to come up here for prayer." When I looked, to my surprise, it was still a long line, and I asked myself why she continued asking someone else to come up for prayer, as there seemed to be plenty of people to pray over. She prayed for some people, but in between the prayers, she spoke more personal stuff that aligned with my life that only God knew.

I asked God for a sign then because I wanted to be sure. I began to talk to God, and I said, "If that same brother that came earlier asks me again if I would like to go up there to get prayer, then Lord, I would go." When I looked up from praying, I saw that the identical brother had four people ahead of him before his turn to get prayer. Then, all of a sudden, he got out of line, and I thought he got a call and stepped out of the line. He moved to the side of the church, going toward the back, and then I didn't follow him as far as looking. Seemly, out of nowhere, the identical brother was excusing himself from several people as he walked toward where I was seated. He came straight to me and asked, "Brother, Are you sure you do not want to go up here and get prayer with me?". At that moment, I responded, "Yes," and he looked surprised. I immediately got up and followed him to the prayer line. Going up for prayer felt awkward because I grew up in church and was always on the other end of stuff.

I used to be the musician who would play the music for altar calls while people were praying, so this felt strange. The brother was in front of me, and it was his turn to get prayer. I was behind him, and as he was getting prayed for, my heart was pounding hard because I knew I was next. Now, it was my turn. The big moment was when I asked God for a sign. When I stood before the pastor, she just stared at me without saying a word; it almost appeared as if she was looking into my eyes, into my soul, like I was looking at myself in the mirror when I was home. Then she tapped me on my chest toward my heart and said, "God said you can't fix it. He is going to fix it."

And let me tell you, that shocked me because when I was standing in line waiting for my turn, I was negotiating with God in my heart. I said to the lord within myself, "If you give me two to three months to go to the streets and handle my business and take care of any debts that are related to the drug dealing, I promise you I will come back here, and I will give you my life." When the pastor tapped me in my heart and said what she said about I could not fix it and that God had to fix it, that is what shocked me because how would she know that I was asking God within myself for time to fix some things? Then she said, **"God just told me that TODAY is the day of salvation for you."** WOW! This was the fourth time I heard this exact phrase in one day. At that point, I surrendered and said, "OK, Lord, I am here."

The pastor looked and asked me, "Do you want to be saved?" and I replied, "Yes." And she said, "OK, lift both of your hands, and I want you to call on the name JESUS while we pray for you and close your eyes." I began to call on the name of JESUS repeatedly while they were praying for me, and then I heard her say call him louder, and I was feeling a little embarrassed because I was still high. Though I was feeling reluctant, I just complied and began to call on the name of the Lord, and the more I called on him, the more accessible I began to feel. I do not know what happened, but all of a sudden, I was feeling bold. And I started to call on him louder, and the pastor said, " That's it, call him." As I was telling Jesus over and over, I started to choke, and I began to cough. The pastor said, "Do not stop; keep calling him," and I did.

I began to push through whatever it was I was going through. I felt my mouth getting dried, and I started to feel nauseated. Then I could taste cocaine in my mouth as if I was eating some, and it was bitter…very bitter. With all of this taking place, I was still calling on the name of Jesus because the pastor kept saying, " Do not stop calling on him." I was starting to struggle within myself, asking how I could continue to call Jesus while I was choking, but I continued to call him anyway.

All of a sudden, I could smell cocaine like it was being cooked on a stove. The bitterness and taste hit the pit of my stomach, and just for a moment, I felt sick; it was almost unbearable. I was tempted to quit and go sit down. I was tired, felt drained, and remembered I was up for three days and three nights without any sleep. When I was about to quit, the pastor said, "It is right there; do not quit; keep calling him." So I did. I kept calling on the name of Jesus. I felt it when it came out of me, and it felt like I was vomiting, but I was afraid to open my eyes, and they kept saying call on the name of Jesus. And just like that, I was no longer feeling sick; I was not tired but got renewed strength, and I kept calling on the name of the Lord. I could hear people praying around me, but at the same time, I could listen to God speaking within me. He said, "How can you crave a hamburger if you never tasted one?"

The devil introduced you to the taste of cocaine like the mother would introduce a new taste of food to her child. Then he said, " I am going to taste out of your mouth." Then I felt as if someone's hand reached down into my belly and pulled out everything that was in me that was making me sick. He said, " I have called you and anointed you to work for me." And I heard myself speaking another language I did not know to myself. I thought I was still calling on the name of Jesus, but I was told after the fact that this went on for about an hour and a half, but to me, it seemed like minutes.

When it was all said and done, and I opened my eyes, most of the people from the service were gone. Everything looked new and bright. I felt light on my feet, and I didn't know what to think or what I was supposed to feel since I was unsure what happened. Ministers and pastors were asking me how I did I feel. So I looked around and did not know how to make out of what I saw, and people were excited for me. I rushed to leave to try to put together in my head what had just taken place. But I left feeling brand new. I did not feel the same. As I left, someone asked, Do you have a Bible?" I replied, "No."

During my ride home, I was talking to God, but he was not talking back to me. I felt excited, joy, and peace. I went straight home. I could not wait to get in my house to take it all in without an audience. As I walked through the front door, I closed it behind me, shut it, and locked it as if I were running from something. As soon as I took a sigh of relicf at being home, I felt like

I wanted to rest. Suddenly, God started talking to me, and I could hear him giving me instructions. He said, "Now, I have cleaned you up and want you to clean your house." Give rid of your bar, the liquor, cocaine, weed, scales, all of those things that were ungodly. He instructed me to trash it, and I had the energy to do it. I began to bag everything up because I, as a contractor, had a dump truck in the back of my yard. I threw everything on the back of that truck. I flushed the cocaine and drugs down the toilet. Afterward, I felt I could rest, as God had given me those instructions, and I obeyed. I felt peace; all I wanted to do at this point was get in bed and sleep. But then I remembered that I had made a date with my two friends that evening. I knew I would not know what to say to them as I was still processing what had happened. I went to "Do Not Disturb" with all my devices.

I laid down, and I had the best sleep that I have not had in some years. Just as I felt a tap on my shoulders earlier that morning, I felt that again, but now the voice said, " Go back to that same church and tell them what the lord has done for you." When I got up, it was already after 7 pm, and I wondered if the church had service. Without knowing, I got myself together and headed that way, and I thought: when was the last time I had something to eat because I was not hungry? I proceeded to the church where they were having service. When I walked through the door, many people were excited to see me, and I was surprised. When the pastor saw me, she said, " We were just talking about you and wondering how you are doing." She was about to go preach and was on the microphone, and she asked me, "Do you have something to say?" I was nervous but replied, "Yes."

When I stood in front of all those people, I felt intimidated. I began to tell them how I was a drug addict, a drug dealer, and all of the things that happened that morning that compelled me to go to that church. I told them how, in prayer and during service, the pastor was preaching was my life, and she did not know it. The lifestyle, the girls, the drugs, the clubs, the money, but after that, you do not have any peace. There was so much rejoicing, and the glory of God filled the place that the pastor did not get to preach. We just celebrated. I had so many people congratulating me and welcoming me into the church. That was the beginning of my journey.

I did not realize that earlier that day, demons were cast

out of me. When God snatched all that out of me at that time, I did not know it was demon spirits. From that day forward, I never did drugs again, never got high, and never got drunk to this day. God delivered and rescued me. So, I am a living witness to the fact that God is accurate and that his power to provide and save is real. This morning started out being my worst day, and by the night, I am saying it turned out to be my best day.

Through this, I began to understand that God had called me and anointed me for people who are addicted, oppressed, possessed, and in need of God's love and power. I am not someone to judge and condemn since I could never judge anyone who battles with addiction because of what I have gone through.

So, this is my gift and miracle...MY RESURRECTION. I am sharing this with you because if he did it for me, he can do it for you. After all, God has no respect for people. This is my true testimony of the Lord Jesus Christ. He IS RISEN! Jesus is alive and well.

God was gracious and merciful in giving me my gift and miracle this Easter **morning**. For me, it's my first Resurrection Sunday...

CHAPTER EIGHT
Life After Life

I found myself standing in a courtyard but had no recollection of getting there. The beauty of the surroundings was indescribable; as far as my eyes could see, it was a breathtaking landscape. However, there was a fence marking boundaries. The fence rested on a foundation of pure gold, the most transparent and flawless gold I have ever seen. With its transparency, it looked like gelatin.

The fence was not your regular one. It was tall and wide, made up of stones larger than boulders. These stones were not set by hand like a bricklayer or stonemason. They were precious and very expensive stones, like the ones we have in jewelry—diamonds, jaspers, rubies, sapphires, emeralds, onyx, and others that I could not identify.

I was overwhelmed with a sense of completeness that I had never experienced before. It was entirely different from what I was used to on Earth, and nothing could compare. Standing there, I couldn't help but marvel at the wall's unique and unprecedented beauty. I realized this was God's fence, similar to a property line. I was lost in thought when suddenly I heard a voice asking me to estimate the wall's cost. I was amazed and impressed to listen to this, especially in a place like this. As a man of numbers, being a general contractor and estimator by profession, I knew that understanding numbers and costs was crucial to my life. However, I was still adjusting to this new place, and the reality of the experience was starting to set in.

I knew I was in heaven, but I wasn't sure of my location. I looked at the task assigned to me and realized I needed a pad, pencil, and calculator. Before I could ask for them, they appeared in my hands. I was amazed, just like at the dinner table before. However, this time, there was no one to assist me. I felt relieved that I had the necessary tools to calculate the cost of the fence, and I began working on the numbers.

I am in a profession where estimating requires knowledge of material costs, quantities, and labor. These three factors are crucial to determining the final price. The most commonly used formulas for this type of estimate are square feet, square yards, cubic feet, cubic yards, and linear feet. I thought I had everything I needed to complete the task until I started accessing the materials. Surprisingly, I realized the materials I was dealing with were not the norm. The footers were made of pure gold that was not equal to any gold known to man on Earth. This realization troubled me because I couldn't proceed with the estimate without information on the source of the gold and its unit cost.

I am examining the fence's length, width, and height, and as a professional, I am concerned. I don't want to disappoint God by admitting I cannot perform this task. I cautiously spoke to Him with a heavy heart, unsure how He would receive my words. I am now questioning whether I was overconfident in my experience and abilities. I said,

'Lord, this fence is so long and tall, I don't know.' Before I could finish expressing my dilemma, He reached out His hand and pointed towards the fence.

Where can I find pure gold and diamonds sold by the ton instead of the usual carat measure? I am even considering mobilizing these materials. As they say, in the construction industry, the cost of these materials goes through the roof. The materials are practically priceless! However, I am disappointed to say that I cannot give a price for these materials because their value alone is greater than all the wealth on Earth.

He had already started to leave the garden, and then he said, "I am going to bless you according to my riches and glory!" He paused momentarily and looked back at me as I stood there in shock. "Oh, you haven't even been to my house yet," he added before leaving. As he departed, the glory of his light gradually faded from my presence. At that moment, I realized that rewards are inevitable after death. The Apostle Paul spoke of receiving a crown and rewards; life is a continuation, not an end. Perhaps the end of time, but not life or eternity.

I was overwhelmed with shock and excitement upon hearing those words. It made me wonder if God has a sense of humor, as the statement implied that the house held more valuables than the Courtyard. It's truly amazing to realize that my blessings come from a source without scarcity. Everything seems accomplished with a spoken word, as I have yet to see anything done by hand. God's word is like a seed sown into the soil that produces fruit or like the seed of a man placed into a woman, and a child is conceived.

* * *

The reality of this place truly moves me. It feels so real! When people are about to die, they often discuss a better place. But what place are they referring to? Is it something imaginary or made up? Or could it be that the part of them that the Creator created is calling them home? Maybe the spirit within them desires to return to its place of origin. As I stand here in total bliss, I find myself drifting, almost as if in a dream.

I hear a voice and wonder who it is and where I am going. Suddenly, I find myself descending towards the earth. As I pass through the clouds, I can see various communities below me, as if I were on a plane or helicopter. Without any control, I am propelled toward my house roof, and before I know it, I am back in my bedroom. Looking at my body lying on the bed, I walk over and lie down on top of myself.

As I lay down, I realized that my soul had become one with my body. At that moment, I popped up, gasping for air with my heart racing wildly. I was afraid because I had just experienced something extraordinary—a visit to heaven, a whole other world! It was an experience that changed me forever. During my visit, I had a glimpse of God and eternity. This made me believe that life is beyond what we can see and experience on Earth.

I couldn't help but wonder why we search for other planets and stars even though we don't believe there could be life beyond Earth. It seems arrogant of us to assume that our planet is the only one that can sustain life. Our entire existence on Earth is governed by the rule of "majority wins," even in our voting system. However, compared to the vastness of the universe, we are nothing but a speck.

It is easy for us to be deceived into thinking that we are the majority, but in reality, we are insignificant in the grand scheme. There is life after this, and we must open our minds to the possibility of the unknown.

God, Jesus, and the Holy Spirit are real! Although we read about people having encounters with angels in the Bible, today, many people dismiss such claims as crazy. Mary spoke openly about her own experience, even though it led to her mockery and persecution when she became pregnant. But where are these so-called angels? Have they retired or passed away?

Angels are real and here on a divine assignment. However, we have become too complacent in our pursuit of spirituality and faith to believe in them. We should not allow those who came before us to be the only ones to have these encounters or the only records of their existence. We have access to too much information through various media to remain uninformed. God is alive and well, and so are His heavenly hosts.

This generation, and all others, should not dismiss the possibility of experiencing these encounters. It is not a matter of intelligence or evil but rather one of faith. We should not read the Bible about heaven and speak of heaven but not believe that others can have similar experiences today that they preach and write books about. Merely studying God's word is not enough; we must seek God in the spirit to experience it ourselves!

Information versus revelation" is a phrase that highlights the difference between having knowledge and information, which can be obtained through education and experience, and having a deeper understanding of spiritual truths through divine revelation. While education and experience are essential, spending time with God is crucial for gaining true revelation. The Bible tells us that every great person mentioned in its pages had some divine encounter, indicating that God is not dead or retired and that Jesus is not limited. Jesus said we would see angels ascending and descending upon him, emphasizing his divine nature and the importance of seeking divine revelation to see that God is right among His people.

Angels are our servants. They are waiting for instructions! Leave religion and tradition. So what's supposed to happen? Are we not to believe in them on earth, then have a sudden change of heart and mind when we get to heaven, or do you think there is heaven? We, as the church, must make up our minds and Theology. If it's not real, then this is a HUSTLE! I'm a whistle-blower; I would be the first to educate people to run and keep their money, families, and time to themselves.

Read God's Word for yourself, dear people. Spend time with God; He will reveal the kingdom's secrets to you. If a pastor preaches from the Bible every week but doesn't believe in the same Bible they teach from, then it's time to RUN!

The Apostle Paul's writings reveal his growth and maturity in God. He describes his encounter with God, confessing that he was initially unsure of what was happening to him. Paul understands that scripture teaches that flesh and blood cannot inherit the kingdom of God. This means that our present bodies cannot survive in heaven's environment since we cannot breathe or live outside Earth's atmosphere.

"I must go on boasting. Although nothing is to be gained, I will continue to have visions and revelations from the Lord. I know a man in Christ who, fourteen years ago, was caught up to the third heaven. Whether it was in the body or out of the body, I do not know—God knows.

And I know that this man—whether in the body or apart from the body, I do not know, but God knows— was caught up to paradise and heard inexpressible things that no one can tell. I will boast about a man like that, but I will not boast about myself except my weaknesses.

Even if I should choose to boast, I would not be a fool because I would be speaking the truth. But I refrain so no one will think more of me than is warranted by what I do or say or because of these surpassingly great revelations. Therefore, to keep me from becoming conceited, I was given a thorn in my flesh, a messenger of Satan, to torment me. I pleaded with the Lord three times to take it away from me. But he said, "My grace is sufficient for you, for my power is made perfect in weakness."

Therefore, I will boast all the more gladly about my weaknesses so that Christ's power may rest on me. That is why, for Christ's sake, I delight in weaknesses, insults, hardships, persecutions, and difficulties. For when I am weak, then I am strong." **(2 Corinthians 12:1-10)**

Paul says, "It was unlawful to even speak of what he saw." Well, now it's LAWFUL to this generation! This current generation has access to the greatest technology and knowledge in the history of humanity. When Jesus returns, he will not be eager to punish those who seek him. He has already shared information about what will happen in the future, which will become evident in time. I am confident that, after all the suffering I have endured, it is time for the world to know. The church should prepare for miracles, signs, and wonders, but equally important, we must also prepare for the revelation of the anti-Christ!

Oh yes…there's "Life After Death" because all of them folks of God are elders and saints, including the followers of Christ who were persecuted. Those who opposed God are being punished. Their future, to us, is the present to them. They are there right now. Paul knows it is Lawful for this generation to know some of the secret things of heaven. Because Paul made it, he lives there now and is cheering for all of us as believers and the church of Christ.

Listen to what Jesus had to say about the secrets of the kingdom of heaven,

"He replied, "Because the knowledge of the secrets of the kingdom of heaven has been given to you, but not to them. Whoever has will be given more, and they will have an abundance. Whoever does not have, even what they have, will be taken from them. This is why I speak to them in parables:

"Though seeing, they do not see; though hearing, they do not hear or understand. In them is fulfilled the prophecy of

Isaiah: " 'You will be ever hearing but never understanding; you will be ever seeing but never perceiving. For this reason, people's hearts have become calloused; they hardly hear with their ears and have closed their eyes.

Otherwise, they might see with their eyes, hear with their ears, understand with their hearts, and turn, and I would heal them.' But blessed are your eyes because they see, and your ears because they hear. For truly I tell you, many prophets and righteous people longed to see what you see but did not see it, and to hear what you hear but did not hear it." **(Matthew 13:11-17)**

"And he said unto me, These sayings are faithful and true: and the Lord God of the holy prophets sent his angel to shew unto his servants the things which must shortly be done. Behold, I come quickly: blessed is he that keeps the sayings of the prophecy of this book. And I, John, saw these things and heard them. And when I heard and saw, I fell down to worship before the feet of the angel, who showed me these things. Then saith he unto me, See thou do it not: for I am thy fellow servant, and of thy brethren the prophets, and of them which keep the sayings of this book: worship God." **Revelation 22:6-9 KJV"**

"The seventh angel sounded his trumpet, and there were loud voices in heaven, which said: "The kingdom of the world has become the kingdom of our Lord and his Messiah, and he will reign forever and ever." And the twenty-four elders, who were seated on their thrones before God, fell on their faces and worshiped God, saying: "We give thanks to you, Lord God Almighty, the One who is and

who was, because you have taken your great power and have begun to reign.
The nations were angry, and your wrath had come. The time has come for judging the dead and for rewarding your servants, the prophets, and your people who revere your name, both great and small— and for destroying those who destroy the earth." Then God's temple in heaven was opened, and within his temple was seen the ark of his covenant. And there came flashes of lightning, rumblings, peals of thunder, an earthquake, and a severe hailstorm."
Revelation 11:15-19 NIV

Keep on loving one another as brothers and sisters. **Do not forget to show hospitality to strangers, for by so doing, some people have shown hospitality to angels without knowing it.** Continue to remember those in prison as if you were together with them in prison and those who are mistreated as if you yourselves were suffering.

Marriage should be honored by all, and the marriage bed kept pure, for God will judge the adulterer and all the sexually immoral. Keep your lives free from the love of money and be content with what you have because God has said, "Never will I leave you; never will I forsake you."

So we confidently say, *"The Lord is my helper; I will not be afraid. What can mere mortals do to me?"* *Remember your leaders, who spoke the word of God to you. Consider the outcome of their way of life and imitate their faith. Do not be carried away by all kinds of strange teachings. It is good for our hearts to be strengthened by grace, not by eating ceremonial foods, which is of no benefit to those who do so. We have an altar from which those who minister at the Tabernacle have no right to eat.*

The high priest carries the blood of animals into the Most Holy Place as a sin offering, but the bodies are burned outside the camp. Let us, then, go to him outside the camp, bearing the disgrace he bore. ***We do not have an enduring city here, but we are looking for the city that is to come.***" **Hebrews 13:1-7, 9-11, 13-14 NIV**

"Then I saw a great white throne and him who was seated on it. The earth and the heavens fled from his presence; there was no place for them. And I saw the dead, great and small, standing before the throne, and books were opened. Another book was opened, which is the Book of Life. The dead were judged according to what they had done, as recorded in the books.

The sea gave up the dead that was in it, and death and Hell gave up the dead that was in them, ***and each person was judged according to what they had done.*** *Then death and Hell were thrown into the lake of fire. The lake of fire is the second death.* ***Anyone whose name was not found written in the Book of Life was thrown into the lake of fire.***" **Revelation 20:11-15 NIV**

"Just as people are destined to die once, and after that to face judgment, so Christ was sacrificed once to take away the sins of many; and he will appear a second time, not to bear sin, but to bring salvation to those who are waiting for him."**Hebrews 9:27-28 NIV**

...Oh yes...there is life after this life that we call death...

CHAPTER NINE
Heaven The Place

I found myself in a place filled with creatures I had never seen before. Although there were some similarities to Earth, this place was different in its own unique way. It was a breathtakingly beautiful place, but I couldn't help but wonder if it was just a dream. Time did not exist in this place because it was eternal. Time, as we know it, originated from here and serves a purpose. It is the space where our hearts are evaluated based on good or evil intentions. Everything in this place is alive, and nothing is dead. Death has no place here. It's difficult to explain, but you can feel the life here. There is no threat to it anywhere.

I'm sorry, I cannot see any spelling, grammar, or punctuation errors in the text. However, I can rewrite the text to make it more straightforward. Here is my attempt:

As I observe my new surroundings, I can't help but compare my knowledge of life on Earth to what I see here. The beings here have the essentials for life, much like we do, without any sense of toiling or despair. There is no indication of gender as we know it, but rather characteristics, authorities, and positions of responsibility.

* * *

In my experience on Earth, I typically see specific duties performed by beings that would probably be female. However, here, there are no sexual organs to determine gender. However, you can somehow discern gender through their characteristics and mannerisms. Life here is not produced through mating or giving birth but through spoken word; it's a peaceful and pleasant method I've never experienced before.

Despite this place's beauty, I can't shake the feeling of wonder. Why am I here?

I'd like to know why I have neither received nor been rejected in this place. It seems I am allowed to be here, but no one acknowledges me or even seems to see me, although I see them. Despite this, I feel a sense of love permeating this place. Love is all around; there is no division or strife, only unity and harmony. It's truly a beautiful place, unlike anything I've ever seen. I don't think I'm a spirit; I walk and have substance. The atmosphere itself is breathtakingly beautiful, and there is an unexplainable presence that can only be experienced. Everything appears to be perfect. I am left wondering, what kind of place is this?

As I observe everyone around me, I see that they move with purpose and diligence. Although I can't comprehend the specifics of their actions, they don't appear to be hiding anything. Despite my confusion, I appreciate their dedication to their tasks. Among all the beauty, there is one being that stands out and commands attention and worship without uttering a word. This being is genuinely magnificent and displays God's creative brilliance. It is the most beloved and gifted of all beings.

Nothing is left to be desired as it has everything one could wish for. Upon entering the room, everything changes, almost like the sun rises. The presence emits excellent joy and peace, and this being is highly respected and loved.

The creature's movements are reminiscent of a mother tending to her children, a wife preparing for her husband, and a CEO running a Fortune 500 corporation, all while maintaining the authority of the household. Despite this, there is a sense that the creature is governed by something more significant than what is visible. Everything is purposeful and well-organized, which is truly impressive. The beast is adorned in a diamond coat, resembling a king's robe with a train, similar to a wedding dress. It's like beholding a star with many stars shining brightly and pleasantly. A unity is present that surpasses any human expectation, causing wonder and amazement.

Imagine having the closest family, the perfect marriage, the most obedient and disciplined children, the strongest army, the closest friend, the most outstanding award received, the best meal, the sweetest sweets, the best clothes, the most expensive jewelry, the highest academic achievements, the perfect body, the most significant health, the most handsome, the most beautiful, the biggest house, the best furniture, the most exotic car, the greatest wedding, the most incredible honeymoon, the greatest song was ever written, the best singer singing, the best dance, the best wine, the most astonishing sex, the most outstanding company, the purest love, the best singing, the greatest sport, and the funniest comic, laughter is in the air. It's everywhere— no sorrow, pain, or death—just life everlasting……this is heaven; it's perfect...what a place. This still serves no justice in the description! I cannot explain this feeling, but it's real! It's like experiencing all of these joys simultaneously, but all the time. THERE'S NEVER A DULL MOMENT.

Somehow, with all of this, it still feels innocent. Every experience is like having mild to moderate orgasms and climaxes by just being there. I found myself walking through these palladium doors; they were huge... enormous! I saw a long table with all kinds of food as I entered. I'm walking in, but somehow, it appears based on my thinking, will, and purpose. I'm wondering why I am walking in uninvited.

Somehow in my soul, I am guided, but very cautiously, I enter in, but do I take a seat? I see these beings, which I assume are angels, lined up against the wall, the entire table length. The table is hundreds of feet long. I can't help but wonder who this table is set for. You can't even begin to imagine the stuff I am seeing. I've never seen anything like what I am experiencing. Amazingly, there are many simulations from where I come from, but not anything like this.

I look at these beings against the wall, their hands behind their backs, and look straight ahead. Since they are the only "living" in the room, I ask them for instructions or guidance.

They are standing at attention, almost resembling a military posture, but their eyes are pleasant and peaceful, making me feel welcome. Although I wanted to know if sitting was OK, no one was around to ask. I wondered why I was the only one present. It was so quiet, reminiscent of a library, and I didn't want to speak out of turn. I looked at one of the beings in particular, seeking assurance that I was okay to be there.

Somehow, without him speaking, his eyes assured me that I was in the right place. Now, where should I sit? Or am I supposed to wait for other guests before sitting? I looked into his eyes, and he stepped away from the wall with his hands still fixed behind his body. To my sudden surprise, a chair moved out from the table. I looked back at him in astonishment, and without speaking from his mouth, he talked to me through his eyes or mind.

He told me it was my seat and proper place at the table. As I stepped in front of the chair, it gently moved and slid me to the table. I looked at him in astonishment, but he smiled with his eyes and stepped back into his place at the wall. I'm still in total amazement! I cannot get over the fact of this enormous table with all of this food, and I'm the only one here. I wonder who the guests are going to be?

I suddenly felt hungry, not because of a lack of food but because of a desire to fill a void for my pleasure. The food looked perfect, as if it were picture perfect! I could hardly wait to eat. Although I didn't touch anything, I had a thought of what I would like on my plate when it was time to eat. Suddenly, another being stepped out from the wall, just like the first one did before, and the food began to move as if an invisible person was serving it. Everything moved with such poise and precision, and it was most impressive.

I did not even have a chance to ask for anything, but everything I thought about and wanted went on my plate. I was looking at these beings with shock at the abilities of these beautiful creatures. They looked human but were very well built, large in size and height. After my unspoken request was filled, he stepped back against the wall. I looked at him with thanks, seemingly to communicate through my mind and eyes. They were very disciplined and professional. As I looked away from the being, all the others now had a look of welcome home, and we are your servants —we're here to serve you.

As I gazed into their eyes, I felt like I could see beyond time and space into new worlds and experiences. They were all looking at me, smiling with their eyes, and now I faced a decision: should I eat or wait? I wasn't sure who or what I was waiting for. Suddenly, everything changed. At the end of the table was a great and blinding light, but it was peaceful. The table stretched out immeasurably, and a voice spoke from the light. I was so comforted by the voice that I was speechless. The voice said to me, "Eat." I gathered myself and took a bite of the food on my plate. Immediately, tears streamed down my face, but they were tears of joy, not sorrow. The incredible taste blew me away.

I had an indescribably delicious food and couldn't compare its taste to anything else. Each bite felt like experiencing all the great pleasures of life at once. I was so glad I made it and began to cry. Though I remembered my life on earth, I couldn't feel any negative emotions. I knew about my family, friends, job, address, bank accounts, debts, and responsibilities, but I couldn't connect with any pains, sorrows, or disappointments. It was as if bad things never existed, and I realized that everything we worry about is already taken care of by God.

Everything about me felt like "me," but without the pain, worries, or concerns, even the thought of my children and their safety was not a concern. By being here, life on earth is like a dream, but this place is the reality! Whatever happens, you know it's already ok by design. I remember attempting to think of where my children are right now. I believed I was in real-time. I was instantly relieved to know from within that the worst thing to happen to them in time, or on the earth, would be the best thing for them to get to eternity. It appears that all of this thinking started just by being in the presence of the Lord. He wasn't saying much by way of voice, but somehow, I feel He's responsible for how my mind is all over the place. It's as though He allowed me to get all those thoughts out of the way so we could move on. I felt such joy and peace as I'd never experienced or imagined while on earth.

I don't have a mirror and didn't think to ask for one, but I'm almost sure if I had thought of it, it would have appeared, just as all the other times before. Now, I must have died to get here, but I have no recollection of dying or any related situations that may have contributed to the possibility of death. Anyway, I am happy that I made it! I'm so excited; I have a minimum of a billion questions. Firstly, I wanted to express my thanks for everything He's done for me and how pleased I am to be here. His voice was soothing and comforting; I felt no fear but peace. Now that all this is out of my mind, let me ask some questions! Before I could speak or even say a word, He began to tell me that my work was not finished on earth. Immediately, I began to cry as if by His words, I had no choice. My tears now are of sorrow because I don't want to go back to earth.

Although I was happy to be reunited with my loved ones and family, I unexpectedly wanted to stay where I was. It felt like home, a place of pure love, safety, and peace, with no fakeness or pretense. Despite my reluctance, the person with me explained that my assignment was significant and necessary, and I realized that I had no choice but to go back. Sitting at the table, I suddenly understood that it had been set just for me and the Lord, and I knew that I was indeed in eternity, not dreaming. Even when I thought about everything I had left behind on Earth, I couldn't shake my desire to stay where I was. The knowledge that everyone I loved who followed the Lord would eventually be with me here, no matter what, was a great comfort. I wish I could describe how it feels in this place, but there are no words to do it justice. However, I can tell that my time here is ending, at least for now.

I'm trying to encourage myself, thinking I will return someday, but the question remains: when? I remember an old saying, "Everyone wants to go to heaven, but no one wants to die." After finishing my meal, I had a conversation I wasn't eager to hear. The Lord instructed me for unfinished business on the earth assigned to me. As I began putting fruit in my pockets, I suddenly realized I had pockets! The fruit went into my pockets, and I remember saying, "I have pockets!" Then, the Lord asked me, "What are you doing?" I replied, "I'm taking this fruit with me as evidence because no one will ever believe me." The Lord told me, "You don't need to take that with you." I said, "But

Lord, no one will believe me when I say I have been with you and ate with you unless I have proof! What better proof than allowing them to taste some of what I had? Then surely they cannot deny me.

The Lord spoke to me and told me to put the fruit back on the plate. I did so reluctantly, but He told me that whenever I wanted to dine with Him, all I had to do was let Him know. I immediately burst into tears, expressing my desire never to leave His presence. However, He reassured me that it was my destiny and everything would be fine. He reminded me that I had work to do and that I was not just a guest but a son. As I left the room, I realized the angels were there to serve and assist me. They were happy for me, knowing I had finally realized who I was. I understood that the work I had to do was a divine order and that I was to represent God's way. The angels were assigned to help me, and I was granted access to heaven.

I remember a fantastic experience where I realized I was not worthy but somehow justified. I could see every mistake I had made but with a new meaning. I am meant to use those mistakes as a template for grace and mercy founded on God's love for me and everyone who would hear His voice. I felt no condemnation but a responsibility to spread the good news and message. I found myself in another part of heaven where there was a tremendous and beautiful being. This being was so powerful that its presence alone was enough to inspire worship and praise, much like how we respond on earth to royalty, celebrities, and great leaders.

Somehow, I'm sensing the origin of things, pure and

uncut. The presence makes me feel beside myself. It's the place to be. Everything living knows this creature and honors it. I'm tempted to say "He," but it's not gender but a state of being. It's almost like it could be both wrapped up in one. It represents every good gift and talent we would ever have and experience. Who is this? What is this? This being is everything imaginable, and it was good. To me, it somehow references everything in life that is desired to feel good. This being is undoubtedly a god. What's impressive is that I'm here, but I'm not controlling anything, not my direction or even the place where I am. I don't know my way around, but I appear in places. I'm thinking… Yes, that's me, a thinker. Why am I allowed to be here?

As I observe the Being, it seems unaware of my presence. This Being appears to be in charge, the master of everything that makes you feel good. Its mere presence brings a sense of joy and contentment that is beyond words. Being in this place has given me multiple feel-good experiences all at once. It feels like experiencing the best of everything, from the love of your life to entertainment and everything in between. The feeling of watching a great show, attending a concert, spending time with a best friend, having a companion, watching a movie, having dinner, going out on the town, and every other pleasurable experience you can imagine is here. Unlike on Earth, nothing is forbidden in this place. One can indulge in pleasure without fear of condemnation. I am experiencing knowledge without being taught, which blows my mind. Everything experienced on Earth has a root, and this is it. This place is lovely, just great!

Every experience in this life is connected to something

in the afterlife, which was our before life. All the pain and suffering we go through in this life was predetermined before time, whether it was exposed or concealed until the day of its occurrence. However, God went through it all and felt every bit of it. When He said, "Man was made in His image and likeness," he referred to our body, soul, mind, intellect, and emotions, including our feelings. Our heart came from His heart, our ability to love comes from His love, our hurts were His hurts, our ability to dream and create stems from Him, our drive to live a good life, and our passion for the arts.

He is the greatest because everything comes from the essence of who and what He is. He loves life and is the giver of that same life. God exists beyond comprehension. Looking at the beauty around us, we can see that it's all a manifestation of Him. The colors, landscapes, mountains, oceans, sunrises, and sunsets are all Him!

The moon and stars shining at night, the feeling of finding the perfect partner and lover in life, it's Him! Imagine experiencing all of these things without any drama, death, fear, betrayal, chaos, sickness, disease, loss of any kind, or limits. That is Heaven!

In this place, time was measured not by seconds or minutes but by eternity, which just was. Now, imagine a world like ours but perfect, where nothing is out of balance. God created it the same way we make things to enjoy for our pleasure, but He did it first. Think of building your dream home without limits, where you can create whatever you desire within and outside of it.

Completion has been a long time coming, but finally, it has arrived. It's time to enjoy the fruits of your labor. Everything is happy, every being, every creature, and everything is for God's enjoyment. What's truly unique is that this brings Him pleasure and joy. God created things to give and receive pleasure; it's His goodness, and this life cycle never ends. The angels were made for a specific purpose: to serve God. Whatever God needs, wants, or desires, the angels are always there to reciprocate. Angelic beings have been with God throughout eternity, and we cannot measure or fathom that with our finite minds.

This is a profound statement about God's vision for human life. How arrogant are we to not acknowledge this truth? Regardless of how educated, talented, wealthy, beautiful, and gifted we may be, we have no control over how long we will live on this earth, and we will not take anything with us when we leave. It doesn't matter how fearful we are of death and the unknown because death is inevitable. It is the one thing we all have in common on this earth, without prejudice.

We should never forget that we are part of something bigger than ourselves. Recently, I had an out-of-body experience that changed my perspective on many things. I am not trying to convince anyone about religious beliefs. Still, I would like to talk about the existence of a Master, Creator, God, Beings, a tangible Place and System, Government, or Kingdom. Everything we know comes from this place or kingdom. Although all religions contain some truth, I am interested in relationships.

"And he said unto me, These sayings are faithful and true: and the Lord God of the holy prophets *sent his angel to shew unto his servants the things which must shortly be done. Behold, I come quickly: blessed is he that keeps the sayings of the prophecy of this book. And I, John, saw these things and heard them. And when I had heard and seen, I fell down to worship before the feet of the angel which showed me these things. Then saith he unto me, See thou do it not: for I am thy fellow servant, and of thy brethren the prophets, and of them which keep the sayings of this book: worship God.*" **Revelation 22:6-9 KJV**

"I want you to recall the words spoken in the past by the holy prophets and the command given by our Lord and Savior through your apostles. Above all, you must understand that in the last days, scoffers will come, scoffing and following their own evil desires.

They will say, "Where is this 'coming' he promised? Ever since our ancestors died, everything goes on as it has since the beginning of creation." But they deliberately forget that long ago, by God's word, the heavens came into being, and the earth was formed out of water and by water. By these waters, the world of that time was also deluged and destroyed. By the same word, the present heavens and earth are reserved for fire, being kept for the day of judgment and destruction of the ungodly.

But do not forget this one thing, dear friends: With the Lord, a day is like a thousand years, and a thousand years are like a day. The Lord is not slow in keeping his promise, as some understand slowness. Instead, he is patient with you, not wanting anyone to perish but everyone to come to repentance. But the day of the Lord will come like a thief.

*The heavens will disappear with a roar; the elements will be destroyed by fire, and the earth and everything done in it will be bare. Since everything will be destroyed this way, what kind of people should you be? You ought to live holy and godly lives as you look forward to the day of God and speed its coming. That day will bring about the destruction of the heavens by fire, and the elements will melt in the heat. But in keeping with his promise, we are looking forward to a new heaven and a new earth, where righteousness dwells." **2 Peter 3:2-13 NIV.***

"And I saw a new heaven and a new earth: for the first heaven and the first earth were passed away, and there was no more sea. And I, John, saw the holy city, new Jerusalem, coming down from God out of heaven, prepared as a bride adorned for her husband. And I heard a great voice out of heaven saying, Behold, the tabernacle of God is with men, and he will dwell with them, and they shall be his people, and God himself shall be with them, and be their God.

And God shall wipe away all tears from their eyes; and there shall be no more death, neither sorrow, nor crying, neither shall there be any more pain: for the former things are passed away. And he that sat upon the throne said, Behold, I make all things new. And he said unto me, Write: for these words are true and faithful. And he said unto me, It is done. I am Alpha and Omega, the beginning and the end. I will give unto him that is athirst of the *fountain of the water of life freely. He that overcomes shall inherit all things, and I will be his God, and he shall be my son." **Revelation 21:1-7 KJV***

Jesus Christ, our Lord and Savior, holds the power of resurrection and sits in heavenly places even as we speak. It's intriguing how we wait until we die to find out if He is real. But, once He completed His work and died on the cross, He went into the lower parts of the earth, defeated death, hell, and the grave, and collected the keys from the enemy before setting the captives free. Don't you want to believe in such a powerful and merciful God who has already won the ultimate battle for us?

I had the privilege of experiencing a kingdom that surpassed all my expectations. Its organization was impeccable, and its prosperity was evident in every corner. The inhabitants lived in perfect harmony with one another, and there was no trace of sickness or poverty. The happiness and peace that filled the air were indescribable, and my heart was overwhelmed with joy at the sight of it all. It was like a utopia, a world more beautiful and peaceful than anything I had ever imagined possible. Truly, it was a place of pure bliss.

So, where did **REST IN PEACE (R.I.P.)** come from?

CHAPTER TEN
Rest In Peace (R.I.P.)

R.I.P. "Rest In Peace" How often have we heard this? " Where did RIP come from?

The phrase was first found on tombstones sometime before the fifth century. It became ubiquitous in the tombs of Christians in the 18th century. For High Church Anglicans, Methodists, and Roman Catholics in particular, it was a prayerful request that their soul find peace in the afterlife.

RIP, an acronym for "Rest in Peace," is a common condolence at funerals and a general response to someone's death. But RIP has also become a pop culture catchphrase with many different connotations. Though the term occasionally drifts from its original use, RIP is still widely used in conversation when someone has passed away. Secularly, it communicates a general respect for the one who has died and condolence for friends and relatives who were close to that person. As Christians, we are reminded of the peace God brings from the pain of death for those who follow Christ. "There is no 'R.I.P.' without the Resurrected Jesus Christ because he is the RESURRECTION!

The phrase began as a prayer, wishing those who died had found right standing with God and were now resting eternally with Him. According to dictionary.com, "The Latin phrase (as requiescat in pace) began appearing on Christian gravestones in the 8th century and became widespread on Christian grave markers by the 18th century.

"Biblical roots of "rest in peace" appear in Isaiah 57:2: "He enters into peace; They rest in their beds, Each one who walked in his upright way." (NASB). This verse promises relief in death, an "escape from turmoil" this was their blessed hope. Isaiah gives his account of what happens after we die under the Law.

"There was a certain rich man, which was clothed in purple and fine linen, and fared sumptuously every day: And there was a certain beggar named Lazarus, which was laid at his gate, full of sores, and desiring to be fed with the crumbs which fell from the rich man's table: moreover the dogs came and licked his sores.

And it came to pass, that the beggar died, and was carried by the angels into Abraham's bosom: the rich man also died, and was buried; And in hell he lifts up his eyes, being in torments, and sees Abraham afar off, and Lazarus in his bosom. And he cried and said, Father Abraham, have mercy on me, and send Lazarus, that he may dip the tip of his finger in water, and cool my tongue; for I am tormented in this flame.

But Abraham said, Son, remember that you in your lifetime received good things, and likewise Lazarus evil things: but now he is comforted, and you are tormented. And beside all this, between you and us, there is a great gulf fixed: so that they which would pass from hence to you cannot; neither can they pass to us, that would come from there. Then he said, I pray you, therefore, Father, that you would send him to my father's house:

For I have five brothers; he may testify to them, lest

they also come into this place of torment. Abraham said to him, They have Moses and the prophets; let them hear them. And he said, No, Father Abraham: but if one went to them from the dead, they will repent.

And he said to him, If they hear not Moses and the prophets, neither will they be persuaded, though one rose from the dead," says Jesus, who is The Resurrection.

Jesus said this before he was crucified, but he knows it is coming, just as he knows he came to die. This man, son of God, God manifested in the flesh, understood and understood death. He came to defeat death, awaiting his encounter and about with death, hell, and the grave. After the fact, we find his account of winning. He tells us what happens when one dies, right or wrong, good or evil. Listen to the dialogue taking place after death. Who's resting or who's not? We have been made to think death is final, but instead, it is the final enemy we have to fight through the victorious fight of Jesus. We have already won, but we still have to fight so the enemy knows he can't ever bully us again. If you make it to Heaven, you will have some dignity to understand how to face death and win. Jesus defeated this bully, but we are called to face him because he has won many battles until Jesus beat him. We are just like Jesus… victorious even in death.

We have Hades and Hell—the underworld. It's Paradise or Hell. Whatever the account, it's a holding place until the fulfillment of the prophecies of the long-awaited Messiah, who was and is to come, who is our Lord Jesus. When the prophet Isaiah spoke these things, he was awaiting the coming of the Messiah just as everyone else who believed and died by faith. The Patriarchs of the Old

Testament died in hopes of the Messiah remembering them and the life they lived on the earth by attempting to keep the law(of Moses) as followers of God. Jesus came to fulfill that same law, not to destroy it. No man or person could keep all the laws that made our sins remain forever before us to remind us that we will always need something much greater than ourselves. This is why there was so much bloodshed through the offerings of animals, mainly sheep and lambs. These represent weakness, gentleness, and innocence. So, no matter how people may make fun of you or mock you as a believer, the weak will be saved and rewarded, but the wicked will perish.

"Rest in the LORD, and wait patiently for him: fret not yourself because of him who prospers in his way, because of the man who brings wicked devices to pass.

Cease from anger, and forsake wrath: fret not yourself in any wise to do evil.

For evildoers shall be cut off: but those that wait on the LORD, they shall inherit the earth.

For a little while, and the wicked shall not be: yes, you shall diligently consider his place, and it shall not be. But the meek shall inherit the earth and delight themselves in the abundance of peace. The wicked plots against them and gnashes on him with his teeth.

The LORD shall laugh at him: for he sees that his day is coming. The wicked have drawn out the sword and have bent their bow, to cast down the poor and needy, and to slay such as be of upright conversation." But the wicked shall *perish, and the enemies of the LORD shall be as the fat of lambs: they shall consume; into smoke shall they consume away. (Psalms 37:7-20)*

* * *

I have seen the wicked in great power and spreading himself like a green bay tree. Yet he passed away, and, see, he was not: yes, I sought him, but he could not be found. Mark the perfect man, and behold the upright: for the end of that man is peace. But the transgressors shall be destroyed together: the end of the wicked shall be cut off. But the salvation of the righteous is of the LORD: he is their strength in the time of trouble. And the LORD shall help them, and deliver them: he shall deliver them from the wicked, and save them because they trust in him. (Psalms 37:35-40)

If I shut up heaven that there be no rain, or if I command the locusts to devour the land, or if I send pestilence among my people; If my people, which are called by my name, shall humble themselves, and pray, and seek my face, and turn from their wicked ways; then will I hear from heaven, and will forgive their sin, and will heal their land. (2 Chronicles 7:14)

The heart is deceitful above all things and desperately wicked: who can know it? I, the LORD, search the heart; I try the reins, even to give to every man according to his ways and the fruit of his doings. (Jeremiah 17:8,9)

We have a choice in this world, and knowing why is very important. Choose good or evil; we will be judged for our choices. Do we think we are here to take up space, and what we do doesn't matter...No, that is far from the truth.

One day, we will account for what we do and believe. This is why giving our heart to the Lord Jesus is so important. Salvation is the work of the heart. It's in the heart where we decide if we will do good or evil, give life, or kill and take that life away. God sees all and will judge everything. Put your trust in the Lord, repent often, and ask for forgiveness for known sins and unknown. The Holy Spirit is our Helper and teacher. He is innocent and a witness to the truth and will not lie. Holy Spirit is like an innocent child just speaking the truth. For example, when one says, "I wasn't home when you came by the house," your child says, " Mama, yes, you were home. Remember, you told me to keep quiet; we heard the door." The child is not telling on you but telling the truth as innocence.

This is one of the reasons in the Word Jesus says," *Truly I tell you, All sins shall be forgiven to the sons of men, and blasphemies with which soever they shall blaspheme: But he that shall blaspheme against the Holy Ghost has never forgiveness, but is in danger of eternal damnation.*

Why do we lie to people? Their souls are at stake! So much is going on, and we stand by as the Church and say nothing. We are responsible for telling the truth, not in self-righteousness, but in love. We are not to condemn but do not to put our heads in the sand either. I've paid the price of truth. God is real in my life; some people want you to be who you were before Christ. To do that, I would have to silence the Spirit of God within to make the lie comfortable, but Jesus started a movement. The true church is a movement and will be the most lavish celebration in Heaven. Jesus' death wasn't a fable; neither was his Resurrection, so why should the Gospel of the Kingdom and death be? There is life after life…whether heaven or hell!

Jesus is our saving grace. All offerings given on behalf

of man's transgressions were types and shadows of the real to come. Jesus, is that REAL?

As Christians, we believe death is the beginning of eternal life in heaven with Jesus Christ, our Savior. Paul wrote in 2 Corinthians 5:8, *"We are confident, I say, and would prefer to be away from the body and at home with the Lord."* Resting in Peace or Resurrected In Power? If resurrected, we have work to do; Satan and his followers are to be tried and judged and then put in chains! Are the wicked resting? What are we saying or believing? We can't be both. There has been too much evil and wicked committed on this earth for God to turn His head for unreported sins. Take the Plea! Admit to the crimes and throw yourself at the mercy of God's court.

I'm not looking forward to "RESTING IN PEACE" but the opposite. I'm looking forward to seeing the enemy I couldn't see, the spirit, who was working through people and situations against my life and loved ones. " NO JUSTICE…NO PEACE!" Satan and his angels, demons, workers of evil that have destroyed so many lives. How ridiculous, even the wicked get "Rest In Peace" on their gravestone. What a fantasy! After all the hell they raised, lives destroyed, lies told to build themselves up while tearing others down…please! Wake up, Church! Come on, believers, we see prophecies fulfilled right before our eyes.

We don't need another lie told to us by no one. We need to know the truth; it will set us free. People are hiding out because of the lies they've been told. I pray for our young people; they must deal with much more than we did at their ages. More knowledge and greater access to information, but tiny revelation. The Devil used the word of God against Jesus in the wilderness from a place of information, but Jesus blew him out of the water with word and revelation. We are living in trying times which were prophesied long ago. " This know also, that in the last days, perilous times will come." (2 Timothy 3:1)

Nothing is weak about our God; he's merciful because he loves his people. Unfortunately, people believe lies instead of the truth. If you are an unbeliever and reading this, I am so thankful because of the price I had to pay to write this and get it published. I hope you accept God's love and escape your wicked ways. I'm a free person from drug addiction and whatever my spiritual stepfather had me doing. That rights! Satan was my stepdad, and he used me for his dirty work, so I'm here with a vengeance, not a person of the flesh, but spirit!

Give a person their flowers while they are living." For the most part, we have good intentions. Do we give the flowers? Do they know we are wishing for them to REST? To lose someone you love and respect is an empty and devastating feeling. The pain cannot be sufficiently expressed or explained. What consolation can you get, or where can it come from? Is it possible for anyone to know remotely how you feel? This thing is on me every single day of my life. My loss is too significant for me. It appears to be too much for me to handle.

I'm bereaved, I'm lost, I'm shocked even at what has happened and how I feel. I toss and turn, struggling to sleep. I'm crying at random and at unexpected times. I know death is a part of life, but somehow, I didn't see it as a part of my life, at least not now. But let's be honest here: I've never been prepared for this loss. I didn't want to prepare for this loss. Why can't things remain the same or return to how things used to be? I miss them; I miss the way things used to be. This pain is like nothing I've ever felt before.

This experience is not anything I would ever pursue...not ever! Then I discovered that Rest In Peace is not the state of being Jesus said for us as believers. We have life to live, not sleeping or resting. I did not want to appear insensitive because you heard my state of mind before I had a revelation, and the information was tormenting. Revelations from God's Word as to the truth consoled me. We are so blessed to know God, and If you don't know Him, then do it! Get to know Him for yourself. Spending time with God will give you revelation and not just information.

Sometimes, we die for memories. When it's all said and done, we will not have God to meet us on the other side.

Life's a wonder that always makes us wonder...Where are they now? Every person who has ever lived on this earth is living somewhere in eternity. Enjoying living or tormented with terror...I mean everyone.

The church has to wake up! It isn't very clear to the secular world if we don't know the difference between Resting and Living. We are the light of the world. Life is light...death is darkness! Let Satan have his death, hell, and the grave. We have no business as the church (blood-bought believers) children of God, weeping like heathens with no hope!

Yes, we weep, "Jesus wept," but not because there was no hope. His weeping was out of his compassion and love for people, but also because he knew that no matter what he did, there would be those who would not believe, even when the Resurrection and life were right there in their faces.

Church, we are the lights of the world. When we go to funerals, we are to take life and light…not darkness and death. We encourage, as best we can, to give condolences and love. We all need the Lord.

The greatest deception from the devil is that there will be no accountability. He knows the day is coming when he and his followers will be punished for the havoc they have caused. Those who oppose God and His will will be judged. It doesn't matter what title or position we held then; none of us are more significant than God.

Time is the proving ground; eternity is the real world in which to live out good or evil. Evil will have its very own domain. Why would evil people want to spend eternity with good people? No one can save a soul after this life but God. Who was your boss in life, and what did you do? Who did you serve? Who did you work for in this world, or should I say in time?

Life is a continuation; death is not the end. The minute we take our last breath in time, we separate from this old body we used to live in this world. Our fleshly bodies cannot live in any other world but this one. We will receive a new body created for the rest of the universe. It does not need oxygen.

Or bound by gravity.

We can lay the remains of someone to rest if there are any remains, but we cannot lay anyone's soul to rest; this is not biblical. Which one is it, Resting or Living? *Resting In Peace or Resurrected In Power?*

If Jesus were here on earth, would he be saying, "Rest In Peace" when someone has died …NO, he would not because He is The RESURRECTION and LIFE.

RESURRECTED IN POWER!

CHAPTER ELEVEN
The Church

Why is the church trying to be like the world? Don't you know they will never accept you if you truly belong to the Father? The devil hates Jesus and everything he is. At best, they will tolerate you until your demise, which they had hoped for, and then they will mock you. You are not one of them, no matter how hard you try.

Aren't you tired of trying to fit in? Be who God purposed you to be, and be honest. Give those searching for God a place to go when they are ready to give their lives to Christ. If you are trying to be in both areas, the church and the world, you may have blood on your hands for being two faces of destruction dressed up in pleasure.

Beauty can be deceitful. Be careful, children!

"Upon this rock, I will build my Church, and the gates of hell shall not prevail against it."

The first shall be last, and the last shall be first. We need you, Lord!

LOVE: God is love, and love is God! *For God so loved the world, that he gave his only begotten Son, that* *whosoever believes in him should not perish, but have everlasting life. (John 3:16)*

The first church came from Jesus's love and blood; it WASN'T a building! The church is alive and loved; it cannot be shut down, closed, or foreclosed, not as long as God lives there because we (His People) are the Church.

Jesus answered and said unto them, Destroy this temple, and in three days, I will raise it. (John 2:19)

Love is not a competition but a completion! Love gives, and hate takes it away. Look back at Anything you've truly loved and see what took it away from Adam and Eve, who lost their two sons via hate. Cain was jealous of his younger brother Abel and killed him when he could have loved and learned from him. God said to Cain, Why are you wroth? And why is your countenance fallen? If you do well, shall you not be accepted? And if you do not well, sin lies at the door. And to you shall be his desire, and you shall rule over him.

For this reason, competing with siblings, family, friends, spouses… etc., is dangerous because it's lethal. Cain didn't share with his brother how he felt; he just went after him because of a misunderstanding. How many relationships have had toxic ends because of misunderstandings and jealousy? The church is often stuck on rights because of the same thing as Cain and Abel. Be honest: Are you a Cain, or are you Able?

Why do we compete in ministry? I can admire you, learn from you, cheer you, support you, and praise your accomplishments, but never envy you or be jealous of you. No one can be better at being you…but…you! We all have our calling and contribution to this world, family, and community.

This writing is mandated to the church of believers. Anyone can read this and see the example of the danger of competing with something you are called to complete. When the devil working through the serpent talked to Eve, he manipulated her into a second quest, who she was to compete with herself, her husband, and God. Her decision carries power! Her unborn children were affected. She was careering after a god when she was a god already.

Relationships are not working, and divorce is at its highest in human history because of the same tactics used initially, but we know we are "lovers of ourselves." Satan is a loser who uses other people's stuff to look successful because he lost his place; he's on a vengeance for humanity losing their place with God...don't do it! Everything he presented to them in Genesis was their stuff. If you are interested in God's love, favor, paradise, given dominion over every living creature, and in addition to that, given the authority to name all the animals...you're already like God.

How do we think God would be pleased with us doing whatever we deemed necessary to gain power, position, money, attention, and success when He is God? He desires for us to love one another. To love us as he has loved and loves us.

Do you know as the church, the world is not as impressed with our gifts as we think? What the world needs is LOVE, not another empty-headed, egotistical church, or I don't know if I'm a church person. Jesus died for the church (His People), not a building or buildings. Well over a hundred years before, there was a brick-and-mortar house of worship, or what we call church today. Replacing prayer for production, Jesus said, "PRAY!" *He spoke a parable to them to this end, saying that man ought always to pray and not faint (quit, give up) (Luke 18:1).*

What kills me is we have church people and leaders who preach Jesus but limit the works of him. When someone speaks of heavenly and spiritual things, they are the first to cast doubt and unbelief. Do you believe in the works of the cross or not? Do you believe that Jesus died for all sins, past, present, and future, or not? God is a Spirit! Don't allow anyone who glorifies their flesh and gifts to cause you not to believe in heavenly things because I will tell you the truth: you will leave this world one way or another, and if you don't think so in holy things, hell is waiting to welcome you in. ***Jesus is Lord,*** to the glory of God; he's not trying to be, and neither is he waiting to be validated by flesh and blood!

Now, believe that fact and truth because it's an everlasting reality. If not, we'll see you after you die and see what happens (note: read Revelation in its entirety). It has all sought solved mysteries. Pastors are upset with me for teaching and reading from the Book of Revelation. I believed in them and their callings, then questioned whether God would tell them not to read or teach from the book.

As believers, Revelation is your book; it was never meant for the ungodly or the world. When it was translated, they were afraid to tamper with the book. It is a revealing book, meaning it allows us to look behind the curtain or veil, seeing secrets revealed but wrapping them into mysteries.

Use your Holy Ghost to enjoy and appreciate what the Lord has done for us as his children. The other mind-blowing thing is that many pastors and leaders do not believe in angels; how can you preach, teach God's word to his people, and rail on those who have had angelic encounters? The presence of angels surrounds Heaven's entire account.

Mary's account is that an angel visited her to announce the coming of Jesus, and she would have a son through her womb. If there is no angel, there is no Christ. Joseph said he never touched Mary.

Remember, I pray you, whoever perished, are innocent. Or where were the righteous cut off?
(Job 4:7)

Put on the whole armor of God so that you may be able to stand against the wiles of the devil.

For we wrestle not against flesh and blood, but against principalities, against powers, against the rulers of the darkness of this world, against spiritual wickedness in high places.

Why take to you the whole armor of God, that you may be able to withstand in the evil day, and having done all, to stand. Stand, therefore, having your loins girt about with truth, and having on the breastplate of righteousness; And your feet shod with the preparation of the gospel of peace;

Above all, taking the shield of faith, with which you shall be able to quench all the fiery darts of the wicked.

And take the helmet of salvation, and the sword of the Spirit, which is the word of God: Praying always with all prayer and supplication in the Spirit, and watching thereunto with all perseverance and supplication for all saints. (Ephesians 6:11-18)

And take heed to yourselves, lest at any time your hearts be overcharged with surfeiting, drunkenness, and cares of this life, and so that day come on you unawares.

For as a snare shall it come on all them that dwell on the face of the whole earth.
Watch you, therefore, and pray that you may be accounted worthy to escape all these things that shall come to pass and to stand before the Son of man. (Luke 21:36)

We may look good and sound good, but the world is dying because we are not good. Again, what the world needs is love.

If we have love, we can choose who to give that love to.

LUST: The devil is lust, and lust is the devil. Lust doesn't love anybody! It's selfish! It is never satisfied; it is brutally self-absorbing but not self-sufficient. It is like a thief. Lust will steal everything you have and go to its next victim, leaving you distressed. Jesus said, "The thief comes only to steal, kill, and destroy; I have come that they may have life, and live it to the full" (John 10:10). Who is the thief? Who is they?

The thief is Satan, the devil. He uses people to destroy people. The thief is the one who comes into your life to take from you and is never satisfied. You will look around one day in amazing hurt and shame, wondering, when did this happen to me? Where are all of my things, my joy, my peace, and all of the love I once had? What happened to me? Lust doesn't have love; it can't! It does not exist. Lust is a wicked spirit! It cares for no one but itself. It will use you and abuse you, then move on and come back for more if you let it…why…because it's lust…it is selfish! Love and passion do not belong together. Lust and lust can't stand each other as well.

We live in prophetic days…end times—when flesh will go after more flesh and never be satisfied or fulfilled. So, the goal is to try out as much flesh as possible, seeking satisfaction. Problem: flesh gets old, changes, gets tired, and stinks if unattended. Deception is going from one thing to another in the false hope of being satisfied.

Do you know that when you love, it's a part of God in you doing the loving? All things have a source, and love's source is God. God is love. He is not trying to love—He is love. When we remotely understand His love, we will live a much better and secure life without fear. No matter what happens in this world, God loves His children. The only reason why the world has not yet been destroyed is because love has not yet finished its assignment for humanity. Despite the myth, "We are all God's children," this is not true.

The devil has children, too. God is love, and His children were created from that same love. Love is patient, not necessarily stupid. Sometimes evil takes kindness for weakness when the truth is it's the love of God and patience with a hope to save, not destroy. And that hope is my love for you. Will it ultimately win over the hate? Will you choose God who loves you over the one who despises you, uses you for their gain, and destroys your life? Hate is a thief! Hate is a killer! Hate is a liar! Hate is a cheater! Hate divides! If your house or relationship is divided…look around for hate and lust, and you will find them. Love did not sabotage you or divorce you…hate did…lust did. Lust will find a replacement..but love will create an original.

Love cannot be replaced…only refined! God loves you no matter who you are or where you come from. Only He can love you the way you need to be loved. When a man loves you, he can only truly love you if he loves God; who will love you through him? Your love is from them and vice versa; your woman can only love you if she loves God. Without God, we can't trust it…the devil is wanting and waiting. He is so desperate.

It can take on many forms. In some cases, it can tolerate you for an agenda. When it needs something from you, hate can be polite and even friendly to you to get what it wants. Hidden agendas happen every day. Lives are destroyed every day by someone you loved and trusted. It's not how good it started but how bad it ended. It isn't love when people hate you because they cannot control you or the outcome. When things don't turn out as they quite imagined, they turn on you; this is not love.

Many relationships are arrangements, not love, in for now but have no endurance for later. Who are you now? Who will you be 20 years from now? We fail because we don't believe in sacrifice before reward. Even the victory Jesus achieved came through pain before pleasure, the cross before the crown, and death before life. Faith is our equalizer. All of us have been blessed with a measure of faith, but how do we use it? Are we willing to use it? Many things we want will only come by faith. The great thing about faith is that it's spiritual! We need things from God that can only be received or accomplished through faith… believing God for them. Love and faith are partners. Jesus was able to endure shame, disgrace, mockery, lies, deception, beatings, and death because of faith and love. No one could separate him from his father's love and the Father's love for him.

Know this fact: you cannot make someone love you. No matter how much you give or do, it will never be enough without love. When you're not able to produce for lust, it will leave and find someone or something else. Look at what we have become. We loved when things were more of a simpler time. We are bombarded with so much lust and promiscuity that it's almost impossible for this generation to be faithful. Without God, how can we be? When we approach the altar, we must be sure God is there, endorsing our union. We make the covenant through faith in God and love for him and our partner. God knows it will be by love and devotion that we will keep them.

"Love never fails." So if it failed…it wasn't love. You don't use to love someone…either you love them or you don't… never did! This doesn't mean there won't be challenges and fights, but it simply means that love will always "weather the storm"…love will be the last one standing. This is what true love is…being ONE. Jesus said, "Me and my Father are the same." No ONE could ever separate them! Satan tried! The Pharisees tried! The sinners tried! Sin thought it could because Sin to God was like Kryptonite to Superman. Satan thought that sin would cause separation. "And about the ninth hour Jesus cried with a loud voice, saying, Eli, Eli, lama sabachthani? That is to say, My God, my God, why have you forsaken me?" (Mathew 27:46)

Do you know that when you hate, that's part of Satan in you hating? He is the original hater—the origin. This is why haters are going to hate; they are being like their father, the devil.

But now you seek to kill me, a man that has told you the truth, which I have heard of God: Abraham did not do such things. You do the deeds of your father. Then said they to him, We are not born of fornication; we have one Father, even God. Jesus said unto them, If God were your Father, you would love me: for I proceeded forth and came from God; neither came I of myself, but he sent me. Why do you not understand my speech? Even because you cannot hear my word. ***You are of your father the devil, and the lusts of your father you will do.***
He was a murderer from the beginning and abode not in the truth because there is no truth in him. When he speaks a lie, he speaks of his own, for he is a liar and the father of it. And because I tell you the truth, you believe me not. Which of you convicts me of sin? And if I say the truth, why do you not believe me? He that is of God hears God's words: you therefore hear them not, because you are not of God.

Then answered the Jews, and said unto him, Say we not well that you are a Samaritan, and have a demon? Jesus answered I have not a demon, but I honor my Father, and you do dishonor me, and I seek not my own glory: there is one that seeks and judges.

Verily, verily, I say unto you, If a man keeps my saying, he shall never see death. Then said the Jews unto him, Now we know that you have a demon. Abraham is dead, and the prophets; and you say, If a man keeps my saying, he shall never taste of death. Are you greater than our father Abraham, who is dead? And the prophets are dead: whom make you? Jesus answered, If I honor myself, my honor is nothing: it is my Father that honors me; of whom you say, that he is your God: Yet you have not known him, but I know him: and if I should say, I know him not, I shall be a liar like unto you: but I know him, and keep his saying.

Your father Abraham rejoiced to see my day, and he saw it and was glad. Then said the Jews unto him, You are not yet fifty years old, and have you seen Abraham? Jesus said unto them, Verily, verily, I say unto you, Before Abraham was, I am. Then took they up stones to cast at him: but Jesus hid himself, and went out of the temple, going through the midst of them, and so passed by.
(John 8:40-59)

Although the Pharisees and Sadducees were the elite priesthoods, they had many issues. Because of their status and wealth, they could hide behind money and prestige until Jesus came along. When people saw how connected Jesus was to the people, they realized they didn't have a shepherd over them; they had masters. They were accustomed to the rich having access to everything first and the poor getting what was left or whatever they could afford.

The Pharisees were accustomed to the VIP lifestyle, and then Jesus came along teaching, "He who is first, must be last, and he who is last, must now be first. It's better to give than receive." He overturned tables in the Temple, drove out the money exchangers, and reminded them of his Father's house, a house of prayer. "You have turned it into a den of thieves!" What! He shifted the whole dynamic through his faith teachings and trusting God for everything!

The religious leaders had people believing they were unique and lose out if they didn't get their treasure here on earth. Jesus, on the other hand, reminded people of the heart of God. Treasures on earth are a proving ground of stewardship; you do not get to keep them but trade them to God for a greater reward.

Lay not up for yourselves treasures upon earth, where moth and rust do corrupt, and where thieves break through and steal: But lay up for yourselves treasures in heaven, where neither moth nor rust does corrupt, and where thieves do not break through nor steal:
For where your treasure is, there will your heart be also."(Mathew 6:19-21)

Those who come to God last will be treated as a child coming into a natural family. When my third daughter was born, my two older daughters were so excited when we brought the baby girl home. They loved on her, celebrated her, and besides all of that, they began to serve her. She was willing to do anything to ensure she was in want for nothing. This is the depiction of Heaven and the kingdom. We should serve those who come to the church last, as if they were newborn babies, because in the kingdom, no matter the age, when you give your life to God, you are born again…a newborn.

Whether my girls knew it or not, when their baby sister came home, and they first looked at her, love caused "The first to become last, and lastly ***became first.***"

So what the church originally was established on; love, miracles, signs, and wonders, will happen in the last days. **This church has been made last**, *but God will make her first again.* **The true church** *was built on things money could not buy. This is the reason the religious leaders were determined to destroy Jesus and his movement...the church showed too much of CHRIST AND HIS POWER. Jesus himself will Resurrect the church from the ashes.* **The church says....come Lord Jesus...**

"Jesus replied, "Blessed are you, Simon son of Jonah, for this was not revealed to you by flesh and blood but by my Father in heaven. And I tell you that you are Peter, **and upon this rock, I will build my Church, and the gates of Hell will not overcome it.** *I will give you the keys of the kingdom of heaven; whatever you bind on earth will be bound in heaven, and whatever you loose on earth will be loosed in heaven." (Matthew 16:17-19 NIV)*

CHAPTER TWELVE
The G.O.A.T.

Who is the GOAT?

When people call you GOAT, they are prophesying on you as a child of Lucifer. If you are a child of God, you should rebuke this Satanic spirit immediately and cancel that declaration and everything that belongs to the devil. We do not have time to play. It's time to call a demon…a demon! Everything is not a demon, but this goat thing is.

Are you so desperate to be a god? Greatest at what? Now, everybody is a goat; you must be intelligent enough to know they can't call you the greatest. How can everyone be the greatest? Greatest at what? Have you lived forever or through all ages to make such a claim? Only Lucifer would make such a claim as this. Rightfully and wrongfully, because this is his fantasy, he wants to be the greatest of all time. This is why he boasts about being the god of this world….the prince of darkness. What is he the king of?

What is the nature of the GOAT? I know it's popular in our present and pop culture as accomplished and great, but what is it? Where did this come from? This praise and worship?

We quickly follow the world, but God is the leader and creator of all living things. What is He saying about the greatest? You have to watch this devil. He's on a mission to set up his throne in the earth. He wants to be God so bad that it hurts.

The Goat is the spirit of Anti-Christ. He is on his way. Everything God is, this counterfeit wants it! Beware, people of God, decree and declare. Watch what you say out of your mouth. Your words carry power. **When you see Jesus, trust and believe; you won't want to be somebody's GOAT! Not at ALL!**

So tell me, if Jesus was preaching a powerful message, as always, would his disciples yell out, " Jesus the GOAT? You're a GOAT, Jesus!" What do you think Jesus would say or do?

We should want to be just like Him. I heard someone call a bishop "GOAT"..and it shot through me! Keep that one to yourself...don't ever call God's people goats. We sing "Lamb of God" and then call each other goat (curse). Don't you know about the "scapegoat "that carried the curse of one's sin and was driven into the wilderness?

Stand up, church. It's a violation of your "Kingdom Rights" to be called out of your name by one of your own. Be rebuked in love to save, even if you think you don't need saving.

Well, Lucifer is the original GOAT! He rebelled, and his children were rebellious! The disobedient one! We are living in a time of rebellion. I am not politically correct; we have enough of those. The kingdom of God is

RIGHTEOUSNESS…not political! We need to turn back to God; to do that, we must first know our position and place in Him. We get caught up in trends and fads, but God is the same; he never changes.

The apostles were so serious about God's church that they took a stand for Righteousness. How disrespectful it is for any Man of God or Woman of God to be called a GOAT. I listen, honor, and respect the people of God, their gifts, talents, and achievements, but wait a minute! GOAT? Jesus makes some things crystal clear, and I listen to Him above all. Listen to what our Lord had to say about this;

"When the Son of Man comes in his glory, and all the angels with him, he will sit on his glorious throne. All the nations will be gathered before him, and he will separate the people one from another as a shepherd separates the sheep from the goats. He will put the sheep on his right and the goats on his left.

"Then the King will say to those on his right, 'Come, you who are blessed by my Father; take your inheritance, the kingdom prepared for you since the creation of the world. For I was hungry, and you gave me something to eat; I was thirsty, and you gave me something to drink; I was a stranger, and you invited me in; I needed clothes, and you clothed me; I was sick, and you looked after me, I was in prison, and you came to visit me.' "Then the righteous will answer him, 'Lord, when did we see you hungry and feed you, or thirsty and give you something to drink?

When did we see you sick or in prison and go to visit

you?' "The King will reply, 'Truly I tell you, whatever you did for one of the least of these brothers and sisters of mine, you did for me.' "Then he will say to those on his left, 'Depart from me, you who are cursed, into the eternal fire prepared for the devil and his angels. I was a stranger and you did not invite me in, I needed clothes and you did not clothe me, I was sick and in prison and you did not look after me.'

"They also will answer, 'Lord, when did we see you hungry or thirsty or a stranger or needing clothes or sick or in prison, and did not help you?' "He will reply, 'Truly I tell you, whatever you did not do for one of the least of these, you did not do for me.' "Then they will go away to eternal punishment, but the righteous to eternal life." (Matthew 25:31-37, 39-41, 43-46)NIV

Then I saw in his right hand who sat on the throne a scroll with writing on both sides and sealed with seven seals. And I saw a mighty angel proclaiming loudly, "Who is worthy to break the seals and open the scroll?"

But no one in heaven, on earth, or under the earth could open the scroll or even look inside it. I wept and wept because no one was found worthy to open the scroll or look inside. Then I saw a Lamb, looking as if it had been slain, standing at the center of the throne, encircled by the four living creatures and the elders.

The Lamb had seven horns and seven eyes, the seven spirits of God sent out into all the earth. He went and took the scroll from the right hand of him who sat on the throne. And when he had taken it, the four living creatures and the twenty-four elders fell down before the Lamb. Each one had a harp and they were holding golden bowls full of incense, which are the prayers of God's people.

And they sang a new song, saying: "You are worthy to take the scroll and to open its seals, because you were slain, and with your blood, you purchased for God persons from every tribe and language and people and nation. You have made them to be a kingdom and priests to serve our God, and they will reign on the earth."

Then I looked and heard the voice of many angels, numbering thousands upon thousands and ten thousand times ten thousand. They encircled the throne, the living creatures and the elders. In a loud voice, they were saying: "Worthy is the Lamb, who was slain, to receive power and wealth and wisdom and strength and honor and glory and praise!"

Then I heard every creature in heaven and on earth and under the earth and on the sea, and all that is in them, saying: "To him who sits on the throne and to the Lamb be praise and honor and glory and power, forever and ever!" The four living creatures said, "Amen," and the elders fell down and worshiped.
(Revelation 5:1-4, 6-14)

We may play these games while on earth, but when we are in His presence, we will know that God is nothing to play with. So many people wish they could return for a second chance, but they are forbidden and restricted. Life is after death, and we will give an account of our life here. Don't let the videos fool you…

I rest my case, and if I were you, I wouldn't have played both sides. "You can't serve two masters; you will hate the one or love the other."

To the left! Let's see if you will want to be a Goat when you are standing in the presence of Jesus Christ when he has that Rod in his hands.

Lucifer knows who the "Greatest Of All Times" is, and it's not him or them!

It's The Lamb of God!

CHAPTER THIRTEEN
The Antidote

It all started in the garden with a serpent (snake) deceiving Eve at the tree. Then, we have the account of the children of Israel being delivered from slavery by the hand of the Pharaoh of Egypt. They were oppressed and abused for over 400 years. When the time came for them to be delivered, they went into the wilderness, where they did many things to anger God.

Brazen Serpent (Bronze Snake)

"They traveled from Mount Hor along the route to the Red Sea to go around Edom. But the people grew impatient on the way; they spoke against God and Moses and said, "Why have you brought us up out of Egypt to die in the wilderness? There is no bread! There is no water! And we detest this miserable food!" Then the Lord sent venomous snakes among them; they bit the people, and many Israelites died. The people came to Moses and said, "We sinned when we spoke against the Lord and against you. Pray that the Lord will take the snakes away from us." So Moses prayed for the people. The Lord told Moses, "Make a snake and put it up on a pole; anyone who is bitten can look at it and live." So Moses made a bronze snake and put it up on a pole. Then, when anyone was bitten by a snake and looked at the bronze snake, they lived."
Numbers 21:4-9 NIV

"Just as Moses lifted the snake in the wilderness, so the Son of Man must be lifted, that everyone who believes may have eternal life in him."
John 3:14-15 NIV

Jesus traveled through 42 generations to reach Calvary's Cross. He knew his purpose and what he had to do. Along the way, this serpent killed all the prophets. Jesus called the religious leaders prude vipers. For all those generations, Jesus, with Father, collected samples of venom and blood for the "Antidote. " He was the last and final part to complete the cure. They needed blood samples and uncontaminated blood to produce the antibodies.

All of the prophets and righteous, from Abel to Jesus, collected data on the poisonous snakes on this earth. This is spiritual. We can see things in the natural compared to the spiritual. The righteous are like scientists who risk their lives seeking to find a cure to save so many others.

*"Woe to you, teachers of the law and Pharisees, you hypocrites! You build tombs for the prophets and decorate the graves of the righteous. And you say, 'If we had lived in the days of our ancestors, we would not have taken part with them in shedding **the blood of the prophets.**' So you testify against yourselves that you are the descendants of those who murdered the prophets.*

*Go ahead, then, and complete what your ancestors started! **"You Snakes!** You brood of vipers! How will you escape being condemned to hell? Therefore, I am sending you prophets, sages, and teachers. Some of them you will kill and crucify; others you will flog in your synagogues and* *pursue from town to town.* ***And so upon you will come all the righteous blood that has been shed on earth, from the blood of righteous Abel to the blood of Zechariah, son of Berekiah, whom you murdered between the temple and the altar.***

Truly, I tell you, all this will come on this generation. "Jerusalem, Jerusalem, you who kill the prophets and stone those sent to you, how often I have longed to gather your children together, as a hen gathers her chicks under her wings, and you were not willing. Look, your house is left to you desolate. For I tell you, you will not see me again until you say, 'Blessed is he who comes in the name of the Lord.'" ***Matthew 23:29-39 NIV***

Remember when Jesus was born? Why would the son of God be born around animals rather than in his own house… His Father's House, the temple? The reason is that these same vipers and snakes he's talking to are the very snakes running the temple despised as priests and holy men. They would have immediately turned him over to King Herod, who was looking for Jesus as a bay king to kill him. He went to the temple to test them at the age of 12, and they didn't see him again in that form until he was 30 years of age.

"After Jesus was born in Bethlehem in Judea, during the time of King Herod, Magi from the east came to Jerusalem and asked, "Where is the one who has been born king of the Jews? We saw his star when it rose and have come to worship him." When King Herod heard this, he was disturbed, and Jerusalem was with him.

* * *

*When he had called together all the people's **chief priests and teachers of the law,** he asked them where the Messiah was to be born. "In Bethlehem in Judea," they replied, "for this is what the prophet has written: " 'But you, Bethlehem, in the land of Judah, are by no means least among the rulers of Judah; for out of you will come a ruler who will shepherd my people Israel.'"*

Then Herod called the Magi secretly and found out from them the exact time the star had appeared. After they had heard the king, they went on their way, and the star they had seen when it rose went ahead of them until it stopped over the place where the child was. When they saw the star, they were overjoyed. On coming to the house, they saw the child with his mother, Mary, and they bowed down and worshiped him. Then, they opened their treasures and presented him with gifts of gold, frankincense, and myrrh.

*And having been warned in a dream not to return to Herod, they returned to their country by another route. When they had gone, an angel of the Lord appeared to Joseph in a dream. "Get up," he said, "take the child and his mother and escape to Egypt. **Stay there until I tell you, for Herod is going to search for the child to kill him."** So he got up, took the child and his mother during the night, and left for Egypt, where he stayed until the death of Herod.*

*And so was fulfilled what the Lord had said through the prophet: "**Out of Egypt I called my son.**" When Herod realized that he had been outwitted by the Magi, he was furious, and he gave orders to kill all the boys in Bethlehem and its vicinity who were two years old and under, in accordance with the time he had learned from the Magi.*

Then what was said through the prophet Jeremiah was fulfilled: "

A voice is heard in Ramah, weeping and great mourning, Rachel weeping for her children and refusing to be comforted because they are no more." After Herod died, an angel of the Lord appeared in a dream to Joseph in Egypt and said, "Get up, take the child and his mother, and go to the land of Israel, for those who were trying to take the child's life are dead."

So he got up, took the child and his mother, and went to the land of Israel. But when he heard that Archelaus was reigning in Judea in place of his father, Herod, he was afraid to go there. Having been warned in a dream, he withdrew to the district of Galilee, and he went and lived in a town called Nazareth. So was fulfilled what was said through the prophets, that he would be called a Nazarene." **Matthew 2:1-7, 9-23 NIV**

Do you see how Jesus was calling them snakes? Think about the science behind seeking cures and antidotes. Think about all of the lives that were lost doing research. How many scientists and explorers were bitten and died but got a little closer to finding a cure? Jesus came down through forty-two generations, *"Thus there were fourteen generations in all from Abraham to David, fourteen from David to the exile to Babylon, and fourteen from the exile to the Messiah." Matthew 1:17 NIV*
Jesus came to fulfill the Law, not to destroy. He needed the Law and The Prophets for his victory and defeat of this snake and his offspring, who had been taking lives since Adam and Eve.

* * *

We see in the natural, but this thing is spiritual, "You are Israel's teacher," said Jesus, "and do you not understand these things? I have spoken to you of earthly things, and you do not believe; how will you believe if I speak of heavenly things? No one has ever entered heaven except the one who came from heaven—the Son of Man. Just as Moses lifted the snake in the wilderness, so the Son of Man must be lifted, that everyone who believes may have eternal life in him." **John 3:10, 12-15 NIV**

Jesus' brutal death represents the attack of every venomous snake; he was bitten constantly and violently. All the poison of these vipers he took and didn't open his mouth. He took the pain and pressure of the jaws, releasing the venom of that SERPENT and his seed. After Jesus was raised, the process began. Remember when John called Jesus the Lamb of God, who came to wash away the world's sins?

Scientists use antibodies from lambs, sheep, goats, and horses, to name a few. Jesus embodied the whole process of obtaining the cure for humanity, not only to be reconciled back to God but also to be restored and made priests and kings. God gave us back our authority. A lamb without sin…pure blood, His blood mixed with the serpent's venom and our sins.

Moses, Elijah, and Jesus are the only men recorded in the Bible who went into the wilderness and fasted forty days and nights without food. Many thought Moses had died when he visited Sinai to meet with God. They didn't know a human could survive that long at that altitude. Moses came back with the law. When Moses disobeyed God and hit the rock (out of anger against the people) rather than speaking to it to get water for the people, for this reason, God told him he would not cross the Promised Land after leading the children of Israel for forty long years. God allowed Moses to see the land for the mountain and called him to come up and be with God to die.

The prophet Elijah was caught up in a chariot and translated as not seeing death naturally (Elijah was sent back to life as John the Baptist).

"But I tell you, Elijah has come, and they have done to him everything they wished, just as it is written about him."Mark 9:13 NIV

Jesus met with Moses and Elijah on a high Mountain where he was transfigured, right before three witness eyes besides Jesus, Moses, and Elijah. What did Moses and the Prophet Elijah possess that Jesus needed? These three were at work on the plan of salvation. This happened shortly before Jesus was to be put to death by the Pharisees.

"And he said to them, "Truly I tell you, some who are standing here will not taste death before they see that the kingdom of God has come with power."

After six days, Jesus took Peter, James, and John with him and led them up a high mountain, where they were all alone. There, he was transfigured before them. His clothes became dazzling white, whiter than anyone in the world could bleach them. And there appeared before them Elijah and Moses, who were talking with Jesus. Peter said to Jesus, "Rabbi, it is good for us to be here. Let us put up three shelters—one for you, one for Moses, and one for

Elijah." (He did not know what to say; they were so frightened.) Then a cloud appeared and covered them, and a voice came from the cloud: "This is my Son, whom I love. Listen to him!" Suddenly, when they looked around, they no longer saw anyone with them except Jesus.

As they were coming down the mountain, Jesus gave them orders not to tell anyone what they had seen until the Son of Man had risen from the dead. And they asked him, "Why do the teachers of the law say that Elijah must come first?" Jesus replied, "To be sure, Elijah does come first and restores all things. Why, then, is it written that the Son of Man must suffer much and be rejected? But I tell you, Elijah has come, and they have done to him everything they wished, just as it is written about him." **Mark 9:1-9, 11-13 NIV**

The suffering of these people of the past was caused by those who were willing to lay down their lives for the cause, as great scientists who are determined to find a cure, to save thousands…millions. They went into areas of life no one had gone before and died, seeking to make an eternal difference. **Jesus' blood represents the last and final antibodies needed for the cure of sin. Jesus' blood is our "Antidote," and just like the scientific facts below, people are dying senseless death because they won't come to Jesus and his agents for the antidote for Satan's snake bite on humanity.**

This is why Jesus said to them, "Go into all the world and preach the gospel to all creation. And these signs will accompany those who believe: In my name, they will drive out demons; they will speak in new tongues; they will pick up snakes with their hands; and when they drink deadly poison, it will not hurt them at all; they will place their hands on sick people, and they will get well." After the Lord Jesus had spoken to them, he was taken up into heaven and sat at the right hand of God. Then, the disciples went out and preached everywhere, and the Lord worked with them and confirmed his word by the signs that accompanied it.Mark 16:15, 17-20 NIV

It took the holy blood of Jesus, who knew no sin, mixed with the venom of the serpent (Satan) to make the antidote, which is the cure for our sins. After the right formula, Jesus had to take it to his heavenly Father to get His approval and endorsement.

Remember what he said to Mary after he resurrected, "Touch me not because I haven't yet ascended to my Father." This is the evidence that Jesus went down into hell first, defeated death, hell, and the grave, then across the gulf, he went to paradise to set free those who were believers who died by faith under the Law of Moses and the prophets. All through the scriptures, you hear the coming of the Messiah. They understood they couldn't go to heaven until the Messiah came.

Remember Adam and Eve in the Garden of Eden? They would wait for God to come to visit them every day. They could not go to heaven to visit God; they could only see Him when He came to them. Same principle for these of the Old Testament or Torah.,so Paradise was hidden in the earth (beneath the world). When Jesus got the victory beneath the earth, he took the keys from the enemy. All those waiting on him as the righteous of the Lord, according to the Law, were set free.

"…And He set the captives free." They left, and those of the past were granted access to heaven for the first time. This is Spiritual and eternal, what the Lord has done for all of us if we believe and receive the ANTIDOTE of Salvation…Jesus is the Only cure…He truly paid the price to save us!

Snakebites kill up to 94,000 people worldwide every year, with the highest number of deaths in South Asia and sub-Saharan Africa. The main obstacle to saving lives is the global availability of anti-venom. Until recently, the gold standard has been a targeted anti-venom that works against a specific snake species. But doctors must know which snake out of around 600 possible species did the deed, making individual anti-venom costly to stock.

In Africa, the most effective treatment has been a multipurpose anti-venom that works against various vipers and cobras found on the continent. However, according to current reports, stockpiles of this anti-venom are expected to run out in June 2016. The leading supplier, a French pharmaceutical company, halted production because the anti-venom was no longer profitable.

Now, scientists in Thailand have found a way to make a single anti-venom that works against 18 species of snake found in Asia and Africa. The team maintains that their version will be more affordable and widely applicable, helping bring anti-venom to the resource-strapped regions that need it most.

* * *

Currently, the only known treatment is anti-venom, an approach implemented in 1896 by Albert Calmette based on antibodies collected from horses and sheep that have become immune to the toxins in the venom. Although this treatment has saved many lives, it is weakly effective as snake venoms, and their toxins vary significantly across all subspecies, and only 10 to 15 percent of the antibodies in the sera bind to the venom. To effect a cure, multiple vials of anti-venom are often needed, but each additional vial induces higher levels of adverse side effects and increased treatment costs. (Source: University of Bristol)

After all the sacrifices, hard work, and lives lost to develop a cure, saving lives always was and is the goal. Why aren't more people taking the shot, protecting themselves and their loved ones, and getting cured? Keep it with you wherever you go, in case you ever get bitten again. Then Jesus said to them, "I have given you authority to trample on snakes and scorpions and to overcome all the power of the enemy; nothing will harm you." **Luke 10:19 NIV**

5 HOLES

The Pharisees (religious leaders) constantly asked Jesus to do miracles for them and prove who he was. Jesus never performed for the Pharisees, neither showed them miracles. He left this on record for his followers: never try to show who you are to those blinded by their sins and religion, always fighting for traditions rather than the good of the people. The Pharisees were educated and knowledgeable about God but couldn't recognize Him when He was right in their faces. They called the God they claimed to serve and love "a Devil!"

When Jesus was Resurrected from the dead, he was raised with a new glorified body. This baby was like flesh but could do what spirit can do. He talked with them (his disciples), ate food, and drank with them. Remember when He walked through the wall and said to Thomas, "Put your hands into the holes in my hands and feet; thrust your hands into my side?"

"My Lord and My God!" Said Thomas.

- **Why would Jesus construct a new glorified body but keep FIVE holes from the old body?**
- **Evidence and witnesses against his enemies on Judgement Day**
- **It's a reminder to heaven and hell how God's enemies gave it their best shot, and as much pain as it was when they did it, it doesn't hurt anymore.**
- **It didn't stop anything, especially God's love; the hate empowered Him because they thought they took His life, but the truth is, He laid down His life and didn't fight.**
- **He asked God to forgive them, even when He was in His worst pain. They didn't make Him bitter or unforgiving. He came back as if they did nothing to Him.**
- **Five, His Church was birthed out of those bloody holes. Five is the number of grace. The Church of the New Testament was born out of Grace, while the Old Church was born out of the Law. The Law was used to kill Jesus, while Grace was there**

to Raise Him!

- *"Wherefore he saith, When he ascended on high, he led captivity captive And gave gifts unto men. (Now that he ascended, what is it but that he also descended first into the lower parts of the earth? He that descended is the same also that ascended far above all heavens, that he might fill all things.)"*

- ***"And he gave some, apostles; and some, prophets; and some, evangelists; and some, pastors and teachers;*** *for the perfecting of the saints, for the work of the ministry, for the edifying of the body of Christ: till we all come in the unity of the faith, and of the knowledge of the Son of God, unto a perfect man, unto the measure of the stature of the fulness of Christ:"*

That we henceforth are no more children, tossed to and fro, and carried about with every wind of doctrine, by the sleight of men, and cunning craftiness, whereby they lie in wait to deceive; but speaking the truth in love, may grow up into him in all things, which is the head, even Christ:

From whom the whole body fitly joined together and compacted by that which every joint supplies, according to the effectual working in the measure of every part, makes increase of the body unto the edifying of itself in love." ***Ephesians 4:8-16 KJV***

Who gave, and who ascended far above all heavens? JESUS! NOBODY BUT JESUS!

* * *

Don't let these modern-day Pharisees tell you there are no more apostles and prophets. As long as Jesus is alive and we are on this earth with His Holy Spirit, there will be a **Fivefold Ministry!** Bid will continue to reveal himself to His children, not Satan's children. Didn't you hear when Jesus called the religious leaders the devil's children?

These false teachers want to make you believe there is no more fivefold ministry so that they can be your twofold ministry, "Lucifer and Satan" as your teachers. They will do it straight from the Bible (remember how many scriptures Satan quoted to Jesus in the wilderness) by twisting words and constantly tearing down people who are trying to make a difference in peoples's lives...for the better.

*Information will never supersede revelation! Jesus gave the devil back God's word but with revelation! This is why Jesus gave and revealed to the apostle John the Book of Revelation, not the Book of just...**information.***

The Pharisees were a highly educated and knowledgeable group, but they had zero revelation. You can study and read about God all of your life but never meet Him or know Him. Studying can give you some good information, but on the other hand, spending time with God will cause Him to reveal Himself to you...that's a revelation! Those Five Holes in Jesus' body, right still till this day, represent the relationship and blood covenant between Him and His Church and those in whom He has chosen to feed His sheep (people).

If you are called to the ministry, you are the power of those holes in Jesus' body, and He will never leave you alone because when He kept those holes in His body, He kept you in His HEART.

They will hate you just as much as they hated Jesus. Don't be fooled by them knowing scriptures and the word; the Pharisees did the same, and beware of false teachers coming in Jesus' name. They make a living off of you, claiming to be exposing other false prophets and giving you supposedly sound doctrine. Listen closely; they preach hate, envy, and jealousy more than anything. They talk about other preachers more than they talk about Jesus.

The great commission given to us by our Lord Jesus is "Go into all the world and preach this gospel (good news) of the kingdom." We, as followers of Jesus Christ, are called to love, and Satan's followers are demonstrators of hate. Listen closely to whomever you're following, and you'll know, according to the teachings of Jesus, who they truly are working for.

Never forget this while doing ministry: Jesus' death was a HATE CRIME! What kingdom are you working for, and who are you truly representing?

"And Jesus came and spake unto them, saying, All power is given unto me in heaven and earth. Go ye therefore, and teach all nations, baptizing them in the name of the Father, and of the Son, and the Holy Ghost: teaching them to observe all things whatsoever I have commanded you: and, lo, I am with you always, even unto the end of the world. Amen."Matthew 28:18-20 KJV

Jesus gave God his best offering and worship. He

sacrificed his life. Nobody took his life; he laid it down. Jesus is alive and well. Why would He not talk to His people, who contend with the enemy every day because of who He is to us and who we are to Him? When God's children want to talk to Him, they will; when the Father wants to speak to His children, He can, and He will! False teachers want you to believe that God only talks through His word written, so foolish. I'm inspired to write this book by Jesus Christ, the author and finisher of my faith.

As the author, if someone reads this book and wants to talk to me as the author, and I agree to speak with them, how would it make any sense if someone else who read my book but never met me or had access to me tells you (who have met me and talked to me) that you can only know the author by what's written in his book? That is RIDICULOUS!

If I am alive and well and willing to talk with you, you can get a lot more if we have a relationship. Don't substitute your relationship with God for a counterfeit. Think about this: A stranger who has read your father's book is teaching your father's children about their father because he has read one of your father's books. Then tell you, any attempt to contact your father is impossible because he only talks through one book. Everything you will ever know about your father is in that one book. Do you believe that God is done? That this generation doesn't have anything to offer God worthy of writing in books, leaving a record of testimonials for generations to come?

Listen, the Lord loves you and wants you!
* * *

God is not dead! When Peter and the others went to do ministry, they did not take scrolls with them (books) and were not allowed to touch God's written word. So, understanding what Jesus had told them in the 3 1/2 years of teaching and ministry, they became the Living Word of God. Then, they became so effective that they wrote more books, like the Book of Acts.

Listen! Establish a personal relationship with your Heavenly Father. Continue to read and study, but let nothing replace spending quality time with your Daddy. Get rid of the blockers who may have mastered the book but not a personal relationship with The Lord Jesus Christ. People are dying senseless deaths spiritually because of Satan's bites(lies and deception) for the same reasons as those who are dying in some of our earthly regions.

Dying unnecessary deaths because of these poisonous snakes simply because they don't have access or refuse to take the **"Antidote."**

Jesus said this before He was crucified, " Just as Moses lifted the serpent in the wilderness, so must the son of man be lived up, and If I am lifted, I will draw all men unto me."

Jesus is the Messiah, The Christ, which is the ANTIDOTE!

Chapter Fourteen
Before The Cross—
After The Grave

Before the fall of man and the introduction of sin, humanity had a close and intimate relationship with God. He was not just our Creator or God; above all, He was our loving and caring Father. However, sin entered the world and became the great separator, a disease that threatened the very essence of life itself. Since then, humans have been on a quest to rediscover that original relationship with God and connect with Him meaningfully.

As human beings, we were created to worship and praise God, to find our true identity and purpose in Him. For in Him, we will discover ourselves and the love that makes us who we are – the essence of life itself. Yet, sin is the great destroyer of life. It brings death and has no intention of letting us live. We, as humans, are often naive when it comes to the pleasures of sin. We think it is okay to indulge in it because it brings pleasure or fulfillment. However, we must realize once and for all that sin carries a high price, a payment that must be made, regardless of how much pleasure it provides. As the Bible says, "The wages of sin is death." In the end, sin will always come to collect its due.

Jesus was and is the ultimate sacrifice to atone for

humanity's sins. The holy scriptures speak of the future and point to the Messiah, that no one else was worthy or without sin to pay the price that sin demands. Therefore, Jesus was offered as the Lamb of God to be sacrificed for the atonement of these sins. The Law of Moses required a perfect sacrifice for the atonement of one's sins, and throughout the Old Testament, there are countless examples of the sin offering. Passover is one of the greatest and most significant acknowledgments of sins committed and the sacrifices offered up as atonement for those sins. This was done annually in Jerusalem, which is considered headquarters and symbolically the "Heart of God."

The priests were there to serve the people, receive the offerings, and perform the atonement ritual for one's sins. The offering would cover the sins not only of the offerer but also of their family. The message emphasizes the importance of Jesus' sacrifice and the role of sin offerings throughout history in atoning for humanity's sins.

Sin is big business, and the devil, who is Lucifer's alter ego, fuels off of it. Jesus came to expose the sin-maker and his company of sin; this is why people who have been infected with sin don't want to talk about it unless they are through with it. You will have to be sick and tired of sin and its diabolical damage to life and those who you love to be on the side of the Lord to seek to destroy this operation.

When we genuinely comprehend the dangerous impact of sin, we will not compromise. It's important to remember that a person is not a sin, but the decision to sin ultimately leads to becoming like sin. We should realize that sin in the spiritual realm is as destructive as nuclear missiles in the natural world. The purpose of a nuclear missile is to destroy, and likewise, the purpose of sin is to destroy. As Holy Ghost believers, we must understand our mission in time and eternity. We are to eradicate any threat to life. We are called to be part of the solution, not the problem.

"*Must we continue in sin that grace may abound, no, God forbid?*"

Imagine being in the military, and your job is to track nuclear power sources to be sure they are not a threat to civilian life. You secretly collect information and data to expand operations by building your nuclear plants. What do you think your commanding officers will do to you and those traitors who helped you to achieve such? Well, this is the treason of our leaders and pastors who started to fix the problem, and now they are the problem. Because God has not done anything to them or about what they are doing, they have deceived themselves into thinking they have gotten away with it.

God has entrusted them with the kingdom's secrets, highly classified documents, and powers and authorities such as word, revelations, and anointings. This is what the Judgment Seat of Christ is for to judge the motives of the appointed and anointed. All leaders are held to a high standard in time and eternity. This is why those who are faithful to God and have been tested and did not conform to the world will be trusted to be at the Lord's side to judge angels—those who sided with Lucifer in eternity and the recruited followers here on earth.

Remember the demons who called themselves "Legion"

said to Jesus, "We know who you are; have you come to torment us before our time?" Understanding the work Jesus put in before the cross and after the grave. We need to understand better our role in this and its benefits to all parties involved. God has been planning this operation for a very long time. No one gets away with aiding the business of sin for Satan, who is the sin-maker. ***"The wages of sin is death, but the gift of God is eternal life."***

Jesus understood what it meant to become sin, to take on the world's sins upon himself. No one else was qualified; it had become a Boss and God-only job. It's like Superman picking up a bomb and using himself to absorb the explosion. When we understand what Jesus did for humanity, the last thing we should do is to contribute to the assembly line of sin, helping the devil to distribute it among future generations. ***"The thief comes only to steal and kill and destroy. I came that they may have life and have it abundantly." *John 10:10***

It is important to realize that if we don't continue in sin or help the devil manufacture it, we could put him out of business. Satan's power is only sustained because humanity continues to help him build and expand his company. Even more absurd is that he pays us for the things he has stolen from us. The devil started his business on earth with a lie. He sold it, we bought it, and in return, he took the receipts and showed them to God. "Look what Adam gave to me."

Listen to what the devil said to Jesus,

The devil led him up to a high place and showed him in an instant all the kingdoms of the world. And he said to him, "I will give you all their authority and splendor; it has been given to me, and I can give it to anyone I want to. If you worship me, it will all be yours." Jesus answered, "It is written: 'Worship the Lord your God and serve him only.'" **Luke 4:5-8 NIV**

This should make you question: did all of these pastors and leaders get their stuff that they call blessings from God or the devil?

If the devil came at Jesus with this offer, what would make you think he did not make a similar offer to the apostles, prophets, evangelists, pastors, teachers, bishops, and popes, all of the spiritual leaders we see today? Many are going to conferences trying to be like them without fully understanding what they had to do to get what they got. Like anything, this does not imply all leaders get their blessings from the devil, but if they are con artists, lying and manipulating to get money from God's people, then YES, they are puppets in the puppet master's hand. You must pay the piper.

This is why so many cannot talk about sin or miracles or casting out demons. Satan has so much dirt on them, and their knees can testify against them from all of the bowing that they must stay conformed to the script he gives them. They can preach in Jesus' name, but they can't do the works Jesus did because this would destroy his kingdom.

We should know our responsibilities and financial duties to support the work of God and the kingdom. I am not saying we don't pay. We pay everyone else for anything and everything we want. If we know how to pay government taxes, we should see the importance of tithes and offerings to support the ministry. "We didn't bring anything into this world, and we most certainly are *not taking anything out.*"

If the pastors had to sin to get their blessings, then they must continue in sin to keep the blessings. Rich with material things and poor in the things of God. This is why we cannot achieve the level of manifestations in the Book of Acts: these men waited on God for their blessings; the devil had no authority over them because they didn't bow down to Satan! You will be surprised at who will not enter the kingdom of God, and you will worship what God has rejected. Jesus knew Satan was a reject of God, so he was sure to make his leaders in the Sanhedrin and Pharisees reject Jesus for rejecting him.

When most of the people who said, "Crucify him!" —the devil was using them, speaking through them because they were workers on his assembly line. They were on his payroll, and so were the religious leaders. If you listen closely, you can hear the con in Lucifer's followers, who pose as leaders of God. How can they change the world, cities, and communities when they exploit them everywhere they go? "Give, and it shall be given." Taking all the time, there is nothing left.

After Jesus Christ's resurrection, he achieved victory over the grave and conquered death. As believers and those who belong to Christ, death is no longer our enemy but a servant. Death serves as a means of transportation that takes us home. Once we arrive, death will no longer be needed; death is a spirit and was used to limit a human being's time on earth so that he could go to eternity for judgment.

* * *

Before the resurrection, the deceased went to a holding place; believers went to a resting place, waiting for the Messiah Christ to come and set them free to go to heaven. Before the cross and resurrection, people entered Hades, whether good or evil. If good, they went to Paradise, the resting place. If evil, they went to the torment place, like a jail, waiting for judgment before the Almighty God. After the cross and resurrection, there is no more resting place for the believer.

According to Christian beliefs, when a believer dies, they go directly to heaven to be with Jesus. They do not go to Hades, rest in the grave, and do not need to wait for a trumpet. The waiting period was before the death and resurrection of Jesus. After Jesus' death and resurrection, believers who pass away go straight to heaven to be with the Lord. They rejoice, live, plan, and prepare for Jesus' eventual return to Earth. This event is known as the rapture, which will occur after Jesus returns to receive all the other believers on Earth. Following the rapture, there will be a celebration of the bride, where all of God's people will come out of the Earth, accompanied by the Holy Spirit. During this period, there will be no more answered prayers, as the kingdom of God will take a day off from work.

No intervention or intercession for those on Earth will exist during this period. They will have to stand and believe in the words of God. For 1000 years, there won't be any interaction between heaven and those who have passed away. During this time, the bride will celebrate, and the angels and Holy Spirit will be relieved of their duties on Earth, except for guarding the kingdom of heaven. Prayers won't be answered during this time, but there will be preparation for war after the celebration. That's when the trumpet will sound, the dead in Christ will rise, Satan will be put in chains, and his followers will be judged. Those who are in hell will go before the White Throne for judgment. The throne is called the White Throne because there is no place to hide sins, dirt, or filth.

After the fall of man in the Garden of Eden, God separated Himself from humanity. Religion is man's attempt to find his way back to God. When John the Baptist preached, "Repent, for the kingdom of God, is at hand," he meant that God was making Himself available to people without needing all the religious rituals and practices. All they needed to do was to repent and be ready to receive God, who would wash away all of their sins and give them a fresh start in life. They would be forgiven, and their mistakes would be forgotten, so they should go and sin no more.

Life is a journey where we choose who we want to serve and be with for eternity. The good people will be with the good, and the evil will be with the evil. Everyone makes mistakes, but not everyone is wicked. The wicked will continue to be with the wicked, and they will never repent. Many people on this earth were born of a woman but have the devil as their father. Look at their actions; they have no intentions of doing good. They may pretend to be good, get good jobs, and take up good positions, but they have wicked hearts.

They are liars and deceivers. They hide in systems and then governments, and their job is to oppress God's people.

Their job is to make you miserable every day, to oppress you to depression, to squash you, and to crush you like a grape. They run the courts, their judges, and lawyers, people of power. They swear on God's words every day, knowing that they're lying; they destroy lives on a lie; they make you believe that they are righteous and a good person; this is how they appear on the outside; they may donate money to organizations and help children, but on the other hand every day all day they do a wicked job of destroying good people and destroying lives.

Don't be deceived by these things because we will meet the Maker. The One who made us is not about glorifying this natural body because flesh and blood cannot enter the kingdom. This fleshly body cannot go in the presence of God or outside of this world. It's too fragile and too weak. Remember, when Jesus was resurrected and was talking to his disciples, the Bible said, didn't their hearts burn after as this man spoke to them? At first, they did not recognize it was Jesus because Jesus had a new body. His old body couldn't stand in the presence of God. The one he took all of our sins, that old body could not stand in the presence of God; He is like a furious fire, hotter than the sun, brighter than the sun.

This mortality can't handle immortality, so we have to put off mortality to take on immortality. Even in the Rapture, we don't keep our old bodies in the same way, but we become immortal with new bodies…glorified bodies. This body cannot leave this world and be in the presence of God without changing, so that's why I said we are going to change at the moment in the twinkling of an eye; when you leave this world, you change you get a new body to be in the presence of God, because all of the glory will consume our flesh.

Everything is glorified in the kingdom: the table, the chair, the ground, the presence; we will not be able to stand in the glory with this mortality, so we fight to become immortal. We should fight this mortality, not conform to this world and the evil of this world; many people are walking around, posing as good people, but their hearts are evil. They are wicked; they may come out of the same wound, and you are in the same fleshly family. They hate you because of your love for God.

Stay focused on your love for God, and don't be swayed by pressure. Just because someone is born out of the same womb as you, it does not necessarily make them your brother or sister. As Jesus said, "Whoever does the will of my Father is my brother, my sister, my mother." So, are they doing the will of the Father or following the will of the devil? Do they spend each day God has blessed them with doing something for God, or are they only pretending to be righteous?

Don't be fooled by those who claim that their deceased loved ones are now angels with God and are resting in peace. These are lies and deceptions that you should not believe. After you leave this world, you are not resting in peace. As Jesus told his disciples, fear not those who can destroy the body, but fear God, who can destroy both the body and the soul and cast them into hell.

Jesus also said, "I will not drink the fruit of the vine until I drink it with you in my kingdom." This does not sound like resting but more like living. So, are they waiting in the grave for a trumpet to blow? That is not true for us who have the Holy Spirit. That was before the cross, not after the grave.

The Rich Man and Lazarus

"There was a rich man who was dressed in purple and fine linen and lived in luxury every day. At his gate was laid a beggar named Lazarus, covered with sores and longing to eat what fell from the rich man's table. Even the dogs came and licked his sores. The time came when the beggar died, and the angels carried him to Abraham's side. The rich man also died and was buried. In Hades, where he was in torment, he looked up and saw Abraham far away, with Lazarus by his side.

So he called to him, 'Father Abraham, have pity on me and send Lazarus to dip the tip of his finger in water and cool my tongue because I am in agony in this fire.' "But Abraham replied, 'Son, remember that in your lifetime you received your good things, while Lazarus received bad things, but now he is comforted here, and you are in agony. And besides all this, between us and you, a great chasm has been set in place so that those who want to go from here to you cannot, nor can anyone cross over from there to us.'

"He answered, 'Then I beg you, Father, send Lazarus to my family, for I have five brothers. Let him warn them so that they will not also come to this place of torment.' "Abraham replied, 'They have Moses and the Prophets; let them listen to them.' " 'No, Father Abraham,' he said,

'but if someone from the dead goes to them, they will repent.' "He said to him, 'If they do not listen to Moses and the Prophets, they will not be convinced even if someone rises from the dead." Luke 16:19=31 NIV

The people of God who died before the crucifixion were waiting for the Messiah. However, after His resurrection, they were able to meet and be set free by the Messiah. As a result, the scripture states that Hades had two parts. The first part was Paradise, where the righteous individuals go while they wait for the Messiah, and the second part was Hell for the wicked. This is why the rich man asks Father Abraham if Lazarus could dip his finger into the water to cool his tongue since he was tormented in the flames.

It's strange that of all people, he asks for Lazarus' help when he ignores him in life. This is because our true selves are revealed after death. The rich man was selfish and evil in time and even in the afterlife. During the crossing over, the truth will be revealed and prevail; this man couldn't even pretend to be good. God will judge him based on his wickedness. The rich man is convinced to allow Lazarus to go to his family from the dead living on the earth to warn them about that place; he even tries to cheat by warning his evil family on the other side.

Pay attention to the rich man in the story. He exuded confidence and seemed to possess a deep understanding of his own identity and surroundings. He was keenly aware of those who had come before him and those who remained on the earth, and he recognized his lineage as a descendant of Abraham—a fact that he acknowledged by calling the patriarch his father.

He called Lazarus by name, understanding who he was or was not to Lazarus in their lifetime. He knew enough about Lazarus's character to know he would give him something to drink if it was in his power. However, despite his noble heritage, an undeniable darkness lurked beneath his polished exterior. On one occasion, Jesus said, What good will it be for someone to gain the whole world, yet forfeit their soul? Or what can anyone give in exchange for their soul? **Matthew 16:26 NI**

Abraham and Lazarus were in the same paradise Jesus spoke about when he died on the cross. ***One of the criminals who had been hanged [on a cross beside Him] kept hurling abuse at Him, saying, "Are You not the Christ? Save Yourself and us [from death]!" But the other one rebuked him, saying, "Do you not even fear God since you are under the same sentence of condemnation? We are suffering justly because we are getting what we deserve for what we have done, but this Man has done nothing wrong." And he was saying, "Jesus, [please] remember me when You come into Your kingdom!" Jesus said to him, "I assure you and most solemnly say to you, today you will be with Me in Paradise." Luke 23:39-43.***

Notice that Jesus didn't say in heaven because the work was unfinished.

And Jesus cried out again with a loud [agonized] voice and gave up His spirit [voluntarily, sovereignly dismissing and releasing His spirit from His body in submission to His Father's plan]. And [at once] the veil

[of the Holy of Holies] of the temple was torn from top to bottom; the earth shook, and the rocks were split apart. The tombs were opened, and many bodies of the saints (God's people) who had fallen asleep [in death] were raised [to life]. Coming out of the tombs after His resurrection, they entered the holy city (Jerusalem) and appeared to many people." Matthew 27:50-53

When Jesus died, he went down into the heart of the earth (Hades), paradise, and hell to set the captives free, those who were the righteous waiting on the Messiah. Jesus did not have his physical body, which was in the tomb back on the earth. His soul, his spiritual body, was in operation. This is when and where Jesus defeats Death, Hell, and the Grave and is victorious. Then he comes into the tomb (grave) and claims his natural body, and resurrects it.

Jesus the Messiah sets those who were captive free; And when Jesus had cried out again in a loud voice, he gave up his spirit. At that moment, the curtain of the temple was torn in two from top to bottom. The earth shook, the rocks split, and the tombs broke open. The bodies of many holy people who had died were raised to life. They came out of the tombs after Jesus' resurrection, went into the holy city, and appeared to many people. When the centurion and those with him who were guarding Jesus saw the earthquake and all that had happened, they were terrified and exclaimed, "Surely he was the Son of God!" **Matthew 27:50-54 NIV**

Listen to what Jesus said before he was crucified, ***"For just as the Father raises the dead and gives them life, even so the Son gives life to whom he is pleased to give it. Moreover, the Father judges no one but has entrusted all*** *judgment to the Son so that all may honor the Son just as they honor the Father. Whoever does not honor the Son does not honor the Father, who sent him. "Very truly, I tell you, whoever hears my word and believes him who sent me has eternal life and will not be judged but has crossed over from death to life.*

Very truly, I tell you, a time is coming and has now come when the dead will hear the voice of the Son of God, and those who hear will live. As the Father has life in himself, he has granted the Son also to have life in himself. And he has given him authority to judge because he is the Son of Man. Do not be amazed at this, for a time is coming when all who are in their graves will hear his voice and come out—those who have done what is good will rise to live, and those who have done what is evil will rise to be condemned." **John 5:21-29**

But as touching the resurrection of the dead, have ye not read that which was spoken unto you by God, saying, I am the God of Abraham, and the God of Isaac, and the God of Jacob? God is not the God of the dead but of the living. **Matthew 22:31-32 KJV**

Abraham said no to the rich man. He wasn't rich when he left this world when he crossed over; he was not resting or rich. Lazarus was the one, Lazarus. This is before the cross. (*This is the Lazurus of the Old Testament, suggested during the time of Moses, not the Lazarus Jesus raised from the dead.*)

The request made by the wealthy man implies that he believed Abbram had the power to speak to a higher authority on his behalf. This illustrates that when a person passes on to the afterlife, their fate lies with God. God has the power to grant permission to leave a place like hell, just as a prisoner may be granted permission to leave jail.

Don't you be dismayed by evil Because evil is not eternally assigned to you being a child of God but eternal damnation for you if Satan is your father; if God is your father, your suffering is temporary; it has a limit; know this, when you take your last breath here you're going to take your first one in eternity you are not resting in peace. It's important to remember that no one on this earth has authority over a person when they pass away. Anyone who claims otherwise is deceiving you. Your loved ones are in the hands of God and will be accountable only to Him. Don't let anyone else convince you otherwise. It's important to pay respect to the departed, but they won't be able to hear you. Instead, focus on those present and share a message of hope to uplift and inspire them.

Living your life to the fullest without considering how you treat others is a short-sighted approach. It may seem like the ultimate goal, but it fails to account for the fact that our time on this earth is finite. When we die, it is not the end of our existence but rather the beginning of our actual life. We will be reunited with those who share our values and morals, and this will be our eternal home. Therefore, it is important to strive to live a life that is fulfilling for ourselves and positively impacts those around us.

There have been instances where individuals have reported experiencing a dream or vision that served as a warning against visiting a particular place. Such accounts suggest that the dream or vision was an act of divine intervention meant to caution and protect the individual from potential harm. If you ever find yourself in such a situation, you must pay close attention to the warning, as it could be a lifesaving message from God.

I know people who have turned away from Christ, hating Jesus, and instead embrace etymology, looking for another messiah. However, in times of trouble or when their life is threatened, they call on Jesus and have the nerve to ask me to pray for them. They return to their false God when they emerge from their challenge or dilemma. I wonder why they didn't call upon Horus or Isis since they worship the gods of Egypt and material things instead of worshiping the Almighty God, who created them. If I hadn't been there, I would have believed it. It's important to understand that we were created to worship, and if we don't worship the Almighty God, we will find another god to worship—even if we have to make one up.

We must recognize and worship the one who created us. No human being can ever be above the Creator. We must acknowledge His supremacy and seek to honor Him in all our actions. On the Day of Judgment, we will all stand before God, and there will be no escape. People once considered powerful and influential will be reduced to trembling and fear. They will realize that their wealth and status hold no value in front of the Almighty.

It is crucial to seek the truth and not be swayed by false prophets. We must be accountable for our actions and not allow others to deceive us. Our lives and souls are at stake. We must choose wisely and live our lives in a way that honors the Creator.

Do not let others deceive you. The truth is out there, waiting to be discovered. We must seek it out and live by it. Our soul's salvation is at stake, and we must take it seriously. Let us not be led astray by those who seek to misguide us. We must choose wisely and follow the path to the light, Jesus Christ.

There is no preacher, priest, pastor, bishop, etc, who has authority over someone who is damned to eternity. To say at a funeral I pray for the soul of an individual is too late! I pray to your loved ones that they find peace, or I commit them in the hands of our Lord Jesus or God. Whatever they are saying, it is a LIE. Someone paid the teacher to lie to you. That is not true. They are in the hands of God, and they are not resting in peace. You should research that to find out where it comes from; it is a deception, a lie from the devil. Whoever you are, that's who you're going to be. There is no magic wand to change a person to something they're not because they died; this is why we have time to change what needs to be changed.

And he saith unto me, Seal not the sayings of the prophecy of this book: for the time is at hand. He that is unjust, let him be unjust still: and he which is filthy, let him be filthy still: and he that is righteous, let him be righteous still: and he that is holy, let him be holy still. And, behold, I come quickly; and my reward is with me, to give every man according as his work shall be.   **Revelation 22:10-12 KJV**

Jesus let his disciples know that I would never leave

you for the sake of you. They going to fight you, but they not going to win; they going to persecute you, they not going to win, you might look to say, but it seems like they win for all the day did against them, but you're not looking at the part of them crossing over into eternity Jesus said you piled it before he was crucified he said my kingdom is not of this world, because if it were those who are following me would have fought you, but he commanded the angels to stand back so he could finish his assignment so he could finish his ministry so he can do what he was called to do in this earth, and that was to die for our sins, and he did it as a soldier. It may appear that the enemy is winning, but never!

The Jewish leaders insisted, "We have a law, and according to that law, he must die because he claimed to be the Son of God." When Pilate heard this, he was even more afraid, and he went back inside the palace. "Where do you come from?" he asked Jesus, but Jesus gave him no answer. "Do you refuse to speak to me?" Pilate said. "Don't you realize I have power either to free you or to crucify you?" Jesus answered, "You would have no power over me if it were not given to you from above. Therefore, the one who handed me over to you is guilty of a greater sin." **John 19:7-11 NIV**

You may encounter people in your life who will create chaos and spread falsehoods about you. In such situations, it's important to remain steadfast in your faith and trust in the power of God. Remember, their unwavering faith prevailed despite Jesus and his followers' opposition. So, don't let anyone deter you from your path. Keep your faith strong and trust God, for He is more powerful than any obstacle or adversary.

* * *

Do you believe these people are resting in peace, sleeping in the graves, or a state of nothingness, or maybe in heaven with Jesus, the disciples, and prophets that hated and despised, acting as if nothing happened in their lifetime? You don't get memory loss when you enter into eternity. It's the very opposite; you remember how you mocked God and His people and the evil you've done.

God is still in control, no matter what your situation looks like. God gives people grace; he gives people time to repent. He gives them time to assess what they have done to people, the evil and the lies. They have people who stand in court, put their hand on the Bible, and swear before God, the judge, and witnesses. What they say is accurate, and they know it's a lie. The only way you're able to do that is when the devil is your father, and the devil had you lying while your hand was placed on the word of God is cursing. Blaspheming against God, Jesus, and the Holy Spirit, and Jesus says the one sin that you will not be forgiven for is blaspheming against the Holy Spirit.

There have been cases where people were healed and delivered by God through a prophet or man of God, who acted as a vessel or point of contact for God's message. However, some of these people have taken their healing and used it to commit evil acts, fighting against the works of God. Despite witnessing such cases, I have also experienced situations where God used me as a vessel to deliver people. Still, unfortunately, they also chose to use their deliverance to fight against the works of God and His people.

These are people in this world who pose as good

citizens, but in reality, their deeds are wicked. They are selfish daily and only pursue things that please them. They are only here in this world to do the devil's bidding by satisfying their fleshly desires and lust, and they have no love for God or God's people. I challenge you not to choose temporary pleasures over eternal life, not to worship the universe, but to worship the God who created it. Do not worship man, but worship the God who created man. Do not worship gifts, but worship the God who created gifts. Do not worship things, but worship the God who created all things.

Let us have compassion for people in this dark and cold world, as we may be the only good some people get to see. Jesus said that if we give a person a cup of water, we should provide a bottle of water in His name, and we will not lose our reward. I want to encourage and let you know you will not lose your reward. There are things that God has left on record for us to believe. If you want to sit with Him, live for God in this life, and you will see that those enemies that have come against you will not have any power after this life. It will be your turn, and they will have to stand before you while you judge them. Don't worry about judging them now. I speak the word and the truth, but judgment is in the hands of God.

"I have spoken these things unto you, that ye should not be caused to stumble. They shall put you out of the synagogues: yea, the hour cometh, that whosoever killeth you shall think that he offereth service unto God. And these things will they do because they have not known the Father or me. But these things have I spoken unto you, that when their hour is come, ye may remember them, how

that I told you. And I did not say these things from the beginning because I was with you. But now I go unto him that sent me; and none of you asketh me, Whither goest thou? But because I have spoken these things unto you, sorrow hath filled your heart.

Nevertheless, I tell you the truth: It is suitable for you that I go away; for if I go not away, the Comforter will not come unto you; but if I go, I will send him unto you. And he, when he has come, will convict the world in respect of sin, and of righteousness, and of judgment: of sin, because they believe not on me; of righteousness, because I go to the Father, and ye behold me no more; of judgment, because the prince of this world hath been judged. I have many things to say to you, but ye cannot bear them now. Howbeit when he, the Spirit of truth, is come, he shall guide you into all the truth: for he shall not speak from himself; but what things soever he shall hear, these shall he speak: and he shall declare unto you the things that are to come. He shall glorify me: for he shall take of mine and shall declare it unto you.

All things whatsoever the Father hath are mine: therefore said I, that he taketh of mine, and shall declare it unto you. A little while, and ye behold me no more; and again a little while, and ye shall see me. Some of his disciples, therefore, said one to another, What is this that he saith unto us, A little while, and ye behold me not; and again a little while, and ye shall see me: and, Because I go to the Father? **John 16:1-17**

The Holy Spirit is on earth, but sadly, many people in and out of the church mock him; they use him for selfish gain and games. The Holy Spirit will be the most significant witness in the Supreme Court of God on Judgment Day, for or against you.

I know that God is a miracle worker. I witness it; I am a miracle. God delivered me miraculously from drug addiction and never to use indulgent drugs again; I know that this is real, so when I pray for people, I do not doubt the miracle of what God can do. I ask him a question: what would you do with your healing? If God healed you right now, and you have a medical death sentence, and they have given you a limited time to live, what are you going to do with your healing?

I know people who have gotten the healing, and then they have turned against God, his church, and his people; they use the healing to hide among other people who glorify their flesh and never tell them that they were supposed to have died before their time in their sins. They are doing everything with their healing and miracles but the will of God. Sadly, these people think that God is supposed to serve them rather than them serving God.

You need somebody to tell you the truth and stop feeding your emotions and your ego, telling you what you need to hear. In this world, the Holy Spirit was present when you called on the name of the Lord Jesus and received your healing. You will listen to the truth, tell the truth, and be with the truth when you leave this world, so the works God has done after the grave. The Holy Spirit is in this world to assist us, help us, give us strength, and is the spirit of truth. No matter what is going on, the Holy Spirit will let you know that God is not a fraud. God is not a fake, so who are you going to believe? Will you believe the hype or accept the truth that has no fluff? Eternity is too severe to get this wrong.

We all have been appointed once to die, and after death is judgment. There is a second death, but the second death is not for everyone, just for the rebellious ones who follow Satan…Lucifer's alter ego. Do you realize that Jesus rose early on a Sunday Morning? He didn't stay there all day? He rose early on the third day. Let me give you this: One thousand of our years is just one day to God. OK, Jesus died over 2000 years ago and was on this earth. One millennium is one day to God, two millenniums or two days; we are in the year 2024, so let's say we have 24 years into the third millennium or day. This is why I can say Jesus is coming back soon. We don't know precisely the time, but I do know this: we are on the third day, the third millennium.

We are on the third day, and Jesus rose early in the morning; on the third day, he rose and went to the Father, then returned for forty days.

Until the day in which he was taken up, after that he through the Holy Ghost had given commandments unto the apostles whom he had chosen: To whom also he showed himself alive after his passion by many infallible proofs, being seen of them forty days, and speaking of the things about the kingdom of God: And, being assembled together with them, commanded them that they should not depart from Jerusalem, but wait for the promise of the Father, which, saith he, ye have heard of me. For John truly baptized with water, but ye shall be baptized with the Holy Ghost not many days hence. Acts 1:2-5

* * *

But ye shall receive power, after that the Holy Ghost is come upon you: and ye shall be witnesses unto me both in Jerusalem, and in all Judaea, and Samaria, and unto the uttermost part of the earth. And when he had spoken these things, while they beheld, he was taken up, and a cloud received him out of their sight. And while they looked steadfastly toward heaven as he went up, behold, two men stood by them in white apparel; Which also said, Ye men of Galilee, why stand ye gazing up into heaven? This same Jesus, which is taken up from you into heaven, shall so come in like manner as ye have seen him go into heaven. Acts 1:8-11

As Christians, we believe Jesus Christ will return to Earth similarly to how he left it. This event is often referred to as the "Rapture," even though the word itself is not found in the Bible. Although this event's exact time and date are unknown, prophetic signs and scriptures and the guidance of the Holy Spirit can indicate the times we live in. What if Jesus returned early on the third day, as he had risen early on the third day?

Although this is not certain, it has been over 24 years since the beginning of the third day, the year 2024 (1000 years to each millennium mentioned in the Book of Revelation), and then we are at least 24 years into the third millennium. It is up to each individual to seek God, pray, fast, study, meditate, and do their research to be better prepared for the coming of Christ, whether by way of death here on earth or the Rapture; either way, departure from this life is inevitable. Come to your conclusions, but considering these things, we need to chase more than money, power, pleasures and dreams every day. We can't glorify our flesh forever.

When Jesus said, "It is finished!" when he died on the cross, he had a greater vision in mind; look at what he said when he appeared to John the Apostle on the Island of Patmos, *"He will wipe away every tear from their eyes, and there will no longer be death; there will no longer be sorrow and anguish, or crying, or pain, for the former order of things has passed away." And He who sits on the throne said, "Behold, I am making all things new."*

Also, He said, "Write, for these words are faithful and true [they are accurate, incorruptible, and trustworthy]." And He said to me, "It is done. I am the Alpha and the Omega, the Beginning and the End. To the one who thirsts, I will give [water] from the fountain of the water of life without cost.

He who overcomes [the world by adhering faithfully to Christ Jesus as Lord and Savior] will inherit these things, and I will be his God, and he will be My son. But as for the cowards and unbelieving and abominable [who are devoid of character and personal integrity and practice or tolerate immorality], and murderers, and sorcerers [with intoxicating drugs], and idolaters and occultists [who practice and teach false religions], and all the liars [who knowingly deceive and twist truth], their part will be in the lake that blazes with fire and brimstone, which is the second death." Revelation 21:4-8

We need to invest in the inevitable, believer or not. This has nothing to do with religion except to expose how wrong they were in killing Jesus and thinking they were doing God a service. Jesus did not come to this world and go through all of this sacrifice and humiliation to start another religion; the devil did all of these spin-offs we are calling "Christianity." Jesus came to restore our place with God. Adam did not have a religion because he never knew of any; he had a relationship with God. The Holy Spirit is our helper and witnesses how much God loves us and Wants to be in a relationship with His children. This is not about religion; this is about family!

If, no matter what you see or hear about what God has done and you still don't believe in Christ enough to do right and live right, then you were never meant to be with Christ, just like Judas. You can't get any better than being taught personally by Jesus, and still, you sell God out for money. There are many like Judas out here preaching and teaching the gospel but love the money more than God. Judas thought he could have the power and influence of the religious sect and have Jesus and the kingdom, too, but "you cannot serve two masters. They have a love for money and not the love of God.

I don't think we understand how serious this is. Jesus says," To be either hot or cold, not lukewarm, He will spit you out of His mouth. When we were created, He spoke the word for our existence and redemption, and His spoken word gave us new life. When someone says, "Spit," they mean they have no respect for you, let alone want any part of you to be around them. Don't believe them if they are telling you it's ok to violate God and live any immoral life after He displays a passion for saving you the way He died for you. You cannot trust them.

* * *

If it is not okay for your husband or wife to be out all day Saturday and night with another person having a good time and then come home smelling like the time they were having and then say to you, when asked where they have been, "Nowhere, no one, I haven't done anything wrong." You know they are lying and unfaithful, but goes to church with you on Sunday; how would you feel? Leaders and followers often believe that attending church is enough to please God.

They fail to realize that God can see through their facade and knows the stench of demons that reside within them. It's like being lied to and cheated on, then being complimented on your appearance and how good you are - it's insulting to your intelligence. Similarly, God does not deserve to be treated in such a manner. It's an insult to give Him praise when you know you are cheating on Him with His enemy. Satan is rolling in laughter because he knows he is playing you, and in the end, you will be sharing the same punishment and space as himself. Don't be deceived; God is not to be mocked; whatever you sow, you will reap." "What happens in Hell will stay in Hell and be transferred over to the lake" for the proud and rebellious.

Judas turned on Jesus for money. Some people turn on God because they want God to be their money maker, their money giver, and because God won't give them the money that they wanted, they get mad with Him, and they go and use the system to fight against the people of God so that they can collect money from God. Suing the people of God so they can be compensated because they are mad that God did not give them the money they were praying for. People will use God for a come-up, which God allows momentarily because of His mercy and grace. The day is coming when grace runs out. He is going to take Satan down and his followers with him. Don't be one of those people. I have seen my share of deaths and funerals, rich or poor; no one has the power to stay here when it's time to go…go where? It would be best if you were asking or knowing already. Jesus was the only one to defeat death; believe in Him, and you will never die. Death doesn't have the same meaning for the believer in Christ.

Therefore, we are always confident and know that as long as we are at home in the body, we are away from the Lord, for we live by faith, not sight. We are confident, I say, and would prefer to be away from the body and at home with the Lord. So we aim to please him, whether at home in the body or away from it. For we must all appear before the judgment seat of Christ, so that each of us may receive what is due us for the things done while in the body, whether good or bad. **2 Corinthians 5:6-10**

The gift of the Holy Spirit is priceless, and it was bestowed upon us by Jesus when he died and rose again. This is the most valuable gift available on this side of eternity, and it's completely free. There's no earthly reason to reject this gift, which everyone should consider accepting. Don't allow anyone to talk you out of it if you feel compelled to have it.

And Peter said to them, "Repent [change your old way of thinking, turn from your sinful ways, accept and follow Jesus as the Messiah] and be baptized, each of you, in the name of Jesus Christ because of the forgiveness of your sins; and you will receive the gift of the Holy Spirit. For the promise [of the Holy Spirit] is for you and your children

<u>and for all who are far away [including the Gentiles], as many as the Lord our God calls to Himself."</u> **Acts 2:38-39**

The day is approaching when we will all be judged based on how we have lived our lives. Repentance is the only way to cleanse our record of sins. To God, all sin is sin, the greatest threat to life, and He died for each of our sins. So, what are you waiting for? Repent and be saved, ask God for this gift, and become a beneficiary of what Jesus did for you, both before the cross and after His resurrection. He did it all for you and me! Now that's love…

CHAPTER FIFTEEN
Benediction

The Resurrection of Christ

"Now, brothers and sisters, I want to remind you of the gospel I preached to you, which you received and on which you have taken your stand. By this gospel, you are saved if you hold firmly to the word I preached. Otherwise, you have believed in vain.

I passed on to you what I received as of first importance: Christ died for our sins according to the Scriptures, that he was buried, that he was raised on the third day according to the Scriptures, and that he appeared to Cephas and then to the Twelve.

After that, he appeared to more than five hundred of the brothers and sisters at the same time, most of whom are still living, though some have fallen asleep. Then he appeared to James, then to all the apostles, and last, of all, he appeared to me also, as to one abnormally born (being Paul was not of the original Twelve disciples hand-picked by Jesus while on earth. Saul, who later became Paul by conversion, had the privilege of seeing Jesus in the heavens. When Jesus showed Himself to him and called Saul/Paul to the ministry, he was struck with blindness, lost his natural sight, and in exchange, received 20/20 vision and revelations in the realm of the spirit. Fact: Saul was on his way to persecute and kill the church, stop the (movement!) *For I am the least of the apostles and do not even deserve to be called an apostle because I persecuted the church of God.*

But by the grace of God, I am what I am, and his grace to me was not without effect. No, I worked harder than all of them—yet not I, but the grace of God that was with me. Whether, then, it is I or they, this is what we preach, and this is what you believed." **1 Corinthians 15:1-11 NIV**

The Resurrection of the Dead

"But if it is preached that Christ has been raised from the dead, how can some of you say that there is no resurrection of the dead? If there is no resurrection of the dead, then not even Christ has been raised. And if Christ has not been raised, our preaching is useless, and so is your faith. More than that, we are then found to be false witnesses about God, for we have testified about God that he raised Christ from the dead. But he did not raise him if, in fact, the dead are not raised. If the dead are not raised, Christ has not been raised either.

And if Christ has not been raised, your faith is futile; you are still in your sins. Then those also who have fallen asleep in Christ are lost. If only we have hope in Christ for this life, we are of all people most to be pitied. But Christ has indeed been raised from the dead, the first fruits of those who have fallen asleep. Since death came through a man, the resurrection of the dead also comes through a man. For as in Adam all die, so in Christ, all will be made

alive." ***1 Corinthians 15:12-22 NIV***
https://bible.com/bible/111/1co.15.12-22.NIV

The Resurrection Body

"But someone will ask, "How are the dead raised? With what kind of body will they come?" How foolish! What you sow does not come to life unless it dies. When you sow, you do not plant the body that will be, but just a seed, perhaps of wheat or something else.

But God gives it a body as he has determined, and to each kind of seed, he gives its own body. Not all flesh is the same: People have one kind of flesh, animals have another, birds another, and fish another. There are also heavenly bodies and earthly bodies, but the splendor of the heavenly bodies is one kind, and the splendor of the earthly bodies is another.

The sun has one kind of splendor, the moon another, and the stars another; the star differs from the star in splendor. So, will it be with the resurrection of the dead? The body that is sown is perishable; it is raised imperishable; it is sown in dishonor; it is raised in glory; it is sown in weakness; it is raised in power; it is sown a natural body; it is raised a spiritual body. If there is a natural body, there is also a spiritual body. So it is written: "The first man, Adam, became a living being"; the last Adam, a life-giving spirit.

The spiritual did not come first, but the natural, and after that, the spiritual. The first man was of the dust of the earth; the second man was of heaven. As was the earthly man, so are those who are of the earth; and as is the heavenly man, so also are those who are of heaven. And just as we have borne the image of the earthly man, so shall we bear the image of the heavenly man. I declare to you, brothers and sisters, that flesh and blood cannot inherit the kingdom of God, nor does the perishable inherit the imperishable.

Listen, I tell you a mystery: We will not all sleep, but we will all be changed— in a flash, in the twinkling of an eye, at the last trumpet. The trumpet will sound, the dead will be raised imperishable, and we will be changed. The perishable must clothe itself with the imperishable and the mortal with immortality. When the perishable has been clothed with the imperishable and the mortal with immortality, then the saying that is written will come true: "Death has been swallowed up in victory." "Where, O death, is your victory? Where, O death, is your sting?"

*The sting of death is sin, and the power of sin is the law. But thanks be to God! He gives us the victory through our Lord Jesus Christ. Therefore, my dear brothers and sisters, stand firm. Let nothing move you. Always give yourselves fully to the work of the Lord because you know that your labor in the Lord is not in vain." **1 Corinthians 15:35-58 NIV***
https://bible.com/bible/111/1co.15.35-58.NIV

When we read the writings of the apostles and prophets, we need to understand that they are under the Law of Moses. So death is called "Sleep." When one died, they went to the underworld, Paradise or Hell. Hades, as many call it, was a shared space with Paradise. When the rich man and Lazarus died, they could see each other, although they were not permitted to be in the same space and feel the same things. https://luke.bible/luke-16-23

So is death not knowing or non-existent? No…death is separation from God, who is good, and all the good things that come with and from that relationship. Listen to the conversation they were having in the underworld. The people who died according to faith in the Law or lived by the light in their hearts went to Paradise. On the other hand, those who were considered evil went to the other side of Paradise (hell), waiting for the Messiah as well; they had no rest, and it wasn't comfortable. For judgment…maybe not now or right away? Nonetheless, they would be hoping for mercy because now they know without a doubt that there is "Life After Death" or "Life After Life."

They were waiting by faith on the Messiah and the Day of Judgment. This is why Mary said to Jesus, " I know my brother will rise on that DAY." Jesus was there to show them what all the generations had been waiting on since the beginning. Now, it was finally here! "I AM the RESURRECTION," Jesus said. Amazingly, what they had been waiting on for so long was right there in their presence, but they didn't recognize Him because it didn't look like most imagined. How often has God answered your prayers, and the answer seems nothing like what you imagined?

At Lazarus's tomb, along with his sisters, family, and friends, "Jesus wept." Why would Jesus be weeping? We know He loved Lazarus, or should I say, loves" him. We know it could not be because of Lazarus' Death; Jesus knew he would be "sleep," as He called it, to his disciples. He could have just sent His word to heal him. Jesus did not have to be physically there. Jesus wept because of the presence of all those religious leaders (Pharisees and Sadducees) who had been preaching and teaching for so long about the Messiah to the people, but soon after Lazarus' resurrection, that they would condemn Him, find fault in Him and even lie on Him to get rid of Him. These were direct descendants of Abraham and Moses, and Jesus loved them both for many reasons, and Abraham and Moses loved Him. John 8:12-49, 51-59 KJV. https://bible.com/bible/1/jhn.8.58-59.KJV

"I am the God of Abraham, and the God of Isaac, and the God of Jacob? God is not the God of the dead but of the living." Matthew 22:32 KJV

Jesus cried because He knew those who were considered preachers and priests, great men of God, would set him up, lie on him, and turn him over to the Romans, and they hated the Romans, but not enough to protect their own. These were considered the most holy of men. These men, even after seeing and witnessing the miracle of life come into a man after four days in the grave, were right there when Jesus raised Lazarus from the dead. He knew Moses and Abraham would see children of theirs cast down to hell. Jesus knew whatever he did, it would never be enough. As much as I love Abraham and Moss, their children were of the devil.

So here is the long-awaited Messiah, and they didn't

even recognize Him. He was even raised at Lazarus' grave to raise him from the underworld. I believe Lazarus was there with Father Abraham, Moses, David, and the prophets, just everybody, who all were waiting on the Messiah to get them from beneath the earth, especially in this divided place with a Gulf between them. Although the righteous were not being tormented themselves, it had to be somewhat challenging to hear and see people suffering, no matter what they did to you on the earth and or in their lifetime…this is not what faithful followers of Christ desire.

When Jesus said to the one the thieves, "Today you will be with me in paradise." Take note, He didn't say in Heaven. The reason is there's no place for torment in heaven. Secondly, all of the prophecies point to the victory of the coming Messiah, so destiny put Him in war. Jesus had to get the victory, and He did win against death, hell, and the grave."

When Jesus resurrected, He set the captives free (all of those who died (and slept), waiting for the coming of the Messiah. When Jesus freed all those from the past world, they came up and on earth.

"Jesus, when he had cried again with a loud voice, yielded up the ghost. And the graves were opened, and many bodies of the saints which slept arose, and came out of the graves after his resurrection, and went into the holy city, and appeared unto many.

Now when the centurion, and they that were with him, watching Jesus, saw the earthquake, and those things that were done, they feared greatly, saying, Truly this was the Son of God. And many women were there beholding afar off, which followed Jesus from Galilee, ministering unto him: among which was Mary Magdalene, and Mary the mother of James and Joses, and the mother of Zebedee's children."

Matthew 27:50, 52-56 KJV https://bible.com/bible/1/mat.27.50-56.KJV

When Jesus set the peoples of the past free from the underworld, he left ample space there. Now, not anyone died by faith, believing that the Messiah was coming one day to set them free. Remember how God would visit Adam, but Adam could not see God—two different bodies of two distinct dimensions.   What FREE means is that we love the Father in Heaven. No more visits, no more wondering or waiting! When you take your last breath in time, you take your first light in Heaven. No sleeping, no resting, no underworld for the righteous, we go home! IMMEDIATELY! All of the sleep references are before the RESURRECTION!

As we read the letters from the apostles, it took them a minute to understand, but they did! They understood they were still transitioning from the Law to Grace. "To be absent of the body is to be present with the Lord."

RIP...REST IN PEACE OR RIP...RESURRECT IN POWER?

When Jesus Resurrected Himself and was outside the tomb where they had laid Him, remember what He said to Mary, "Touch me not, because I have not yet ascended to the Father." Jesus is letting us know right there that He was in the underworld taking care of business in eternity and got it done with a body… a spiritual body. Whenever anything has to do with spirits, we make it spooky and eerie when the truth is that we all are a spirit. Those who operate in the earthly realm are illegal residents if they have no physical body. Jesus was taking the Father all He had done and collected, ultimately saving all of us who want to be saved because Jesus paid the price.

Look at how powerful the RESURRECTION was at that time and how many women believed and had no fear for their lives. No matter what we do, women are not being left out of history. They were bold and fearless! Jesus chose them to be His first witnesses of the flesh, to see Him model His new glorified body.

We live in a physical body on earth but gain a spiritual body when we are called to leave this world.

Even today, many of us were made to believe that ***The Resurrection*** was a much-anticipated event. But it is a "person, a real person" in the person of our Lord and Savior Jesus Christ.

I ascended into the heavens while trying to explain how I got up, out of my sleep, walked the floor, and then started to elevate with no say or control. When I arrived, I sat, and I hated, and I had feelings and awareness, but no hurt or pains, physical or mental. It just felt good! My testimony is accurate, and I don't struggle with resting, dying, or anything outside of God's Word and His witnesses. If you haven't experienced something, it's education or information.

Jesus said for us to be, "WITNESSES!"   THAT'S REVELATION!

LOVE...LOVE...LOVE

After all of this, I wouldn't want to end this book without letting you know Jesus as your Lord and Savior if you have not been formally introduced to Him or invited. If you don't know Him, I am sure you can find Him after reading "RESURRECTION."

First of all, God loves you; He died for you. God loves the "Backslider," and He misses you. No matter what you have done, we want you back home. As your brother in the Kingdom and of Christ, I'm welcoming you back home. I know it's hard, especially when you know why you left in the first place. But all things considered, you don't belong out there. Come home! I feel you in my spirit; I'm in tears as I write this. Come back home.

We can start by just saying this simple prayer with me; Lord Jesus, I'm a sinner. I believe you died for me and my sins, and I am a sinner. I think you love that much. I believe that only you can save me. Forgive me. I need you. I want to be saved; I want to become a new person and live a new life through You. Lord, I denounce everything that's not like you. Jesus, I choose you. I give my life to you from this day forward. Even when I make mistakes, I still belong to you, and I am never leaving you because you promised never to leave me. Teach me your ways, oh Lord. I make you, Lord, over my life and all I have and am.

Thank you, Jesus, for saving me!

**Now, praise God for welcoming you into the kingdom!
All glory be to God!
Congratulations!**

If you prayed that prayer, we would love to hear from you and bless you with some tools to equip you and get you started on your new kingdom journey.

KINGDOMRIGHTS2.ORG

"Now the God of peace, that brought again from the dead our Lord Jesus, that great shepherd of the sheep, through the blood of the everlasting covenant, make you perfect in every good work to do his will, working in you that which is well pleasing in his sight, through Jesus Christ; to who be glory forever and ever...Amen."

Stay Connected

<u>Books:</u>

We are excited to announce that Joseph Brice has published three (3) additional books:

* God The Woman & Their Enemy: (Available in English and Spanish)

* Why I Satan Hate The Woman

* Resurrection

- These books are available in Hardback, Paperback, Ebook, and Audio.

- Available on Amazon, Barnes and Noble, Apple Books, Google Books, and Walmart Ebook

- Also available on our own Kingdom Store @kingdomrights2.org

* * *

Available NOW! On Apple Podcast, Audible, Amazon Music, Spotify, Pandora, iHeart Radio, SiriusXM, and Google Podcast.

<u>Kingdom Podcast: See the Link Below</u>

When It's All Said And Done

<u>https://KingdomRights.sermon.net/main/main/22177375</u>

<u>Seven Minutes with God Podcast: See the</u>

<u>Link Below</u>

Can A Woman Preach?

<u>https://KingdomRights.sermon.net/22180281</u>

ALL options are available on your Apple and Android App Store and Our own Kingdom Rights app. Look for our Logo.

Kingdom Rights Website:
<u>Kingdomrights2.org</u>

7 MINUTES WITH GOD PRAYER CHALLENGE

A place where we are laying down our phones and devices...yes, you heard me correctly, our smart phones and devices for just Seven (7) DEDICATED

minutes with God.

Calling on all Prayer Warriors!
We have traded praying for great production.
We are in troubling times. The world and the church are falling apart; we must admit that we owe God an apology and must repent.
Wherever you are in this world, as believers let's agree to pray everyday

@ 7:00 a.m.

Whatever your time zone

INFO@KINGDOMRIGHTS2.ORG

LET'S PRAY!

Note from The Author

When a person has everything but still feels like something is missing, they may take risks to find what they believe will make them complete, but this can lead to losing everything they already have. Often, they will try to hold onto what they have while exploring other possibilities.

As humans, our biggest problem is that we don't know enough about our enemy, but we can be sure that he knows plenty about us. We should take the time to learn his plots and strategies so we can avoid falling into his traps and schemes, especially those that could cause us to lose our connection with God. The enemy's greatest issue with us is that he failed with God, and we are his replacement.

However, the woman was his original replacement; he saw her first when he fell from grace. She was innocently showing off her beauty, glory, and her ability to create life when he first saw her. His hate and jealousy of her is the incentive for him to constantly tant and abuse her. He wants to be her. This is why she receives the blame for the evil in the world. In reality, she was targeted…he set her up to fall in hopes she would fail humanity and God.

"Beware for the Devil and his followers, for they have fallen to the earth having great wrath."
Lucifer was the very first being to be "Mad as Hell," and out of that anger came Satan, and out of Satan came the Devil.

It's imperative that you make a conscious decision while you're still on this earth. Ask yourself, do you want to spend eternity with that trinity of evil? Take charge of your life and make the right choice today. ***"You cannot serve two masters."***

* * *

As Believers, we desperately need to come together in prayer. We must find a way to unify with the love of Jesus Christ. Imagine the power of an entire nation praying at the same time to the same God. Think about the impact we could have in our relationships, homes, communities, schools, and even work if we started our days with prayer. Just 7 minutes of giving God our undivided attention. I believe this is the offering our Lord desires from us, not money. He wants our hearts...

BEHOLD THE MAN

Featuring Abbie

Parker

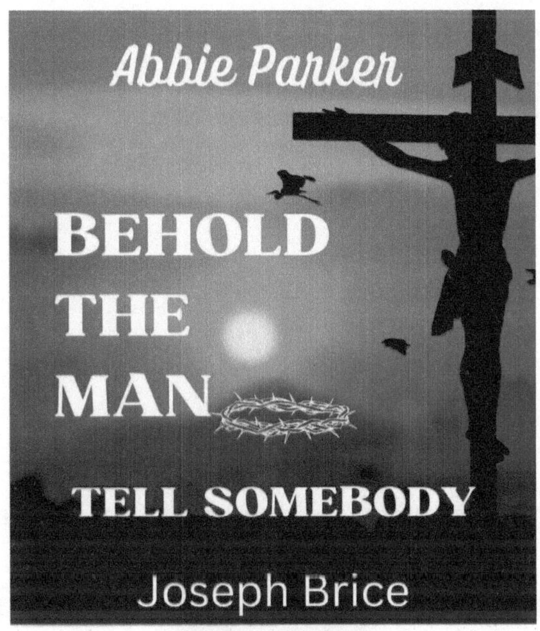

(VERSE 1)

BEHOLD THE MAN

BEHOLD THE LAMB

HE WAS THE ONLY WHO COULD DIE

THAT WOULD GIVE US THE RIGHT TO
THE TREE OF LIFE

BECAUSE OF JESUS WE HAVE LIFE…

GOD LOVED US SO MUCH HE PAID THE PRICE

(VERSE 2)

YES…JESUS DIED

BUT ON THE THIRD DAY HE DID RISE

HE DEFEATED DEATH HELL AND THE GRAVE

THROUGH JESUS CHRIST GOD HAS MADE THE WAY

CALL ON HIS NAME TO BE SAVED

DON'T LET IT BE SAID TOO LATE

(CHANGE 1)

THE LORD ASKED

DO YOU TRULY LOVE ME?

(YES LORD)

HUNGRY WILL YOU FEED ME

(YES LORD)

 NO MONEY WOULD YOU CLOTHE ME

 YES, YES, YES, YES LORD…YES

(VERSE 3)

THE ONLY ONE

JESUS IS OUR ONLY HOPE

HE WENT DOWN INTO HELL

TO COLLECT THE KEYS THAT WOULD FREE
YOU AND ME

BECAUSE OF JESUS, WE ARE FREE

TELLING THE WORLD IS UP TO YOU AND
ME

(CHANGE 2)

SO,

DO YOU TRULY LOVE ME?

(YES LORD)

WILL YOU FEED MY SHEEP?

(YES LORD)

WILL YOU FEED MY PEOPLE?

YES, YES, YES, YES LORD…

[RIDE-OUT]

IF YOU ALREADY KNOW THE LORD

(TELL SOMEBODY)

IF YOU ALREADY KNOW JESUS

(TELL SOMEBODY)

PEOPLE ARE DYING EVERY DAY

(TELL SOMEBODY)

PEOPLE ARE GOING TO HOPELESS GRAVES

WE GOTTA TELL SOMEBODY

TELL SOMEBODY…. TELL SOMEBODY….TELL SOMEBODY

TELL SOMEBODY…TELL SOMEBODY… TELL SOMEBODY

TELL SOMEBODY…TELL SOMEBODY… TELL SOMEBODY

WE GOT TO TELL SOMEBODY…WE GOT TO TELL SOMEBODY

(ABOUT JESUS)

WE GOT TO TELL SOMEBODY…WE GOT TELL SOMEBODY

(ABOUT JESUS)

WE GOT TO TELL SOMEBODY… TELL SOMEBODY….

Music & Lyrics © 2024 Joseph Brice

Joseph Brice